W9-BGW-944

CADET GRAY

A cadet officer (with chevrons) and a Plebe in "50-50" Full Dress, on the Plain at West Point. The officer's insignia denote that he is a Distinguished Cadet, a lieutenant, and a First Classman.

CADET GRAY

PICTORIAL HISTORY OF LIFE AT WEST POINT AS SEEN THROUGH ITS UNIFORMS

FREDERICK P. TODD, COL., U.S.A.R.   ILLUSTRATED BY FREDERICK T. CHAPMAN

© Copyright. 1955.
by STERLING PUBLISHING CO., Inc.

To My Wife

By the Same Author
SOLDIERS OF THE AMERICAN ARMY

Copyright, 1955
by STERLING PUBLISHING CO., Inc.
215 East 37 St., New York 16, N. Y.
*All rights reserved under International
and Pan-American Copyright Conventions*
Manufactured in the United States of America
Library of Congress Catalog Card No. 55-12306

*This edition is published by Bonanza Books,
a division of Crown Publishers, Inc.
by arrangement with the original publisher, Sterling Co., Inc.*

Contents

CREDITS

All photographs were supplied by the United States Military Academy. The prints and objects illustrated are in the West Point Museum Collections, unless otherwise noted.

The spearhead (above) adorns the present Corps Colors. It was presented to the Military Academy in 1928 by the Commonwealth of Massachusetts, and has been polished so often that the plating has been worn down to the brass. (On next page) This 1820 picture is the earliest known drawing of a West Point cadet. He holds the rank of cadet captain, and is posing while the Corps forms in line in the center of the Plain. The buildings in the back are the North and South Barracks, the Academy (or academic building) and the Mess Hall. This print appeared in the *Analectic Magazine,* August 1820.

Preface

In the matter of uniforms, as in other things, West Point has often been a law unto itself. It has met and solved its problems of clothing and equipage pretty much as its successive superintendents have seen fit, and these problems have been quite different from those of the Army at large. Often these solutions have been informally reached and informally acted upon. Documentation is seemingly impossible in some instances and much dependence must be placed on personal memory and pictorial sources.

I am particularly indebted in this work to the researches of my predecessor as director, the late Colonel Allen L. Keyes, who assembled a large amount of material on the cadet uniform in conjunction with Mr. Arthur E. DuBois of the Quartermaster General's Office. Many others have given real assistance, and I want specially to thank: Colonel William J. Morton, Jr., Librarian of the United States Military Academy, and his staff; Colonel R. J. Stillman and his assistants at the Cadet Sales Store; and Dr. Sidney Forman, Archivist of the Military Academy. Many of the pictures used were processed by the Signal Corps Laboratory at West Point, whose chief, Mr. A. A. Kepler, has shown immense care and patience in providing them. Numerous graduates of the Military Academy have passed on to me their personal experiences, and several have read the manuscript in whole or in part. I am particularly grateful to Captain W. L. Frankland, Jr., of the Public Information Office, to Mr. Milton Perry of my own staff, as well as to Mr. Tom Parker for their useful criticisms.

Finally, I am most fortunate in the collaboration of Mr. Chapman on this book. His work has been more the character of co-author than artist.

FREDERICK P. TODD

West Point Museum
West Point, N. Y.

Towering over the Plain today are the Cadet Chapel and barracks, which make a fitting background for this impressive exhibition of the Corps of Cadets on parade at West Point.

The United States Military Academy

The United States Military Academy was established in 1802, more than a century and a half ago, at West Point, New York, on the Hudson River, where the river winds through a chain of mountains called The Highlands — a spot of great natural beauty.

From 1776 to 1781, the British, with armies at both ends of the river, had threatened to capture the entire Hudson Valley, hoping thus to split the United States. Thanks in part to the forts at West Point the British were held in check — a measure which contributed greatly to the winning of American Independence. Protected by almost impassable mountains, West Point commands the river for miles to the north and south. It was a perfect place from which to block an enemy moving along the Hudson in either direction.

The Military Academy of today — a mass of gray stone buildings — is built on one of the bluffs high above the Hudson. Today it accommo-

dates over 2500 cadets who come from all over the United States.

For more than twenty years after the close of the Revolutionary War, West Point remained our most important military post. Here were stored the weapons and supplies made and captured during the War. And here also was stationed the greater part of the United States Army, which in those early days was not very large.

Congress determined in 1802 to provide a regular and permanent military school, administered by the Corps of Engineers, and passed a bill, signed by President Thomas Jefferson on 16 March, which established the United States Military Academy. But establishment and accomplishment were a long way apart. There were some prominent officials who did not approve of the idea and did what they could to obstruct.

Therefore, it was more than ten years before anything like a real school came about.

During the Revolutionary War, the 1700-foot chain shown here was stretched across the Hudson from West Point to Fort Constitution (A) to block ships from passing. Fort Clinton (C) still stands on the West Point Military Reservation.

Before the Academy was established in 1802, boys were trained to become officers by appointing a few at a time to the two Regiments of Artillerists and Engineers of our small Army. There they served in the ranks, learning soldiering the hard way. They were called "cadets," were treated as junior officers, but received the pay of a sergeant. One of their jobs was to carry the battalion colors, a duty performed by ensigns in the Infantry, and by cornets in the Cavalry. Sometimes they were taught a little more than the duties of an officer, but by and large their formal education was meager and they saw very little of a classroom.

Since West Point at this time was such an important military post, gradually the few cadets in the

East were centered there. For example, Joseph G. Swift, the first man to graduate from the Military Academy, was a cadet at Fort Wolcott, in Rhode Island. In October 1801, he was transferred to West Point to complete his military education.

When Swift arrived at what was not yet the "Military Academy" (though some called it that), he found twelve boys there, with one professor. They were of quite different ages: one cadet was only ten. But a start had been made and it was only logical that Congress should choose West Point as the permanent location of the Military Academy. Everything about the school was undeveloped and haphazard, and even after 1802, this condition continued.

From the very first there has never been any discrimination as to race, creed, or color. The second cadet to graduate was a young Jewish boy named Simon Magruder Levy. West Point has had its share, too, of Negroes.

The sole purpose of the Academy is to train

A map of "the West Point in Hudson's River," showing how it juts out to form a sharp angle. On this map Fort Clinton is still called Fort Arnold, a name that was changed after the Revolution, for obvious reasons. Spotted on the bluffs and in the hills are blockhouses and batteries. In the hills near the river are forts, along with the barracks and a blacksmith shop.

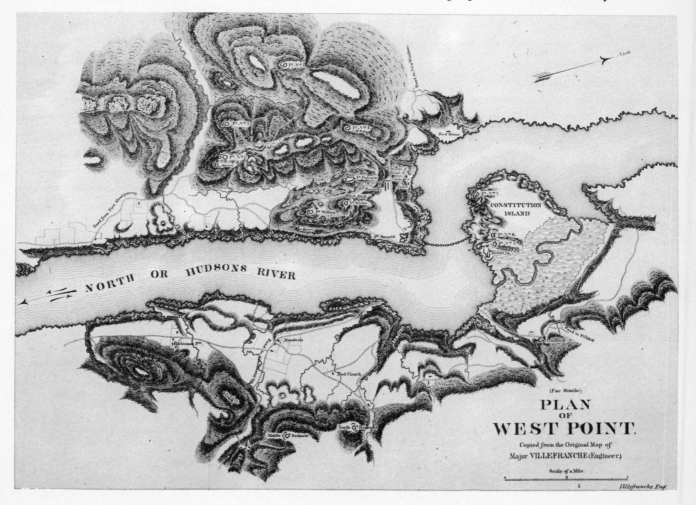

NORTH OR HUDSONS RIVER

CONSTITUTION ISLAND

(Fac Simile)

PLAN
OF
WEST POINT.

Copied from the Original Map of

Major VILLEFRANCHE (Engineer)

Scale of a Mile.

Villefranche Eng.

CADET AND SOLDIERS OF THE REGIMENT OF ARTILLERISTS AND ENGINEERS, 1801

Before the United States Military Academy was established in 1802, cadets, like the one pictured here, were trained to become officers in the Regiment of Artillerists and Engineers of our Army. They wore almost the same uniforms as their fathers who had fought through the Revolutionary War.

cadets to become officers. During their four-year training at West Point they receive regular pay, and upon graduation become officers with the rank of second lieutenant in the United States Army or Air Force.

The life of a cadet at the Point is not an easy one. Yet the fact that each year some 500 men graduate, many with high honors, proves that the work is within the capacity of the average American boy.

Perhaps a "sense of belonging" goes a long way to pull cadets through these tough four years and does much to make this a pleasant as well as an unforgettable experience. For a cadet soon discovers that his "home" is in "*the* Corps," as the United States Corps of Cadets is known to the men who have marched in it.

The Corps! Bareheaded salute it,
* With eyes up, thanking our God*
That we of the Corps are treading
* Where they of the Corps have trod —*
They are here in ghostly assemblage,
* The men of the Corps long dead,*
And our hearts are standing attention
* While we wait for their passing tread.*

The Corps also has its own special uniform. (In the back of this book, in Appendix B, the reader will find a detailed chronology of cadet dress.) That the Corps still wears essentially the same uniform that was worn 140 years ago is proof of the powerful part "cadet gray" has played in the lives of the men who have gone to West Point. When at last the cadet graduates, he carries with him into the Army the strongest memories of his four years — memories of when he "put away the Kaydet Gray" and of the song that went with it.

This song, "Army Blue," is played at Graduation when the First Class (as the senior class is called) steps out of ranks for the final time as cadets. It is, too, always the last dance at "hops." The first verse and chorus is sung to the old tune "Aura Lea":

We've not much longer here to stay,
* For in a month or two,*
We'll bid farewell to Kaydet Gray,
* And don the Army Blue.*

Army Blue, Army Blue,
* Hurrah for Army Blue,*
We'll bid farewell to Kaydet Gray,
* And don the Army Blue.*

One of the blockhouses at West Point, as seen in an 1802 painting by Archibald Robertson. Guard houses like this were erected at strategic spots around the post.

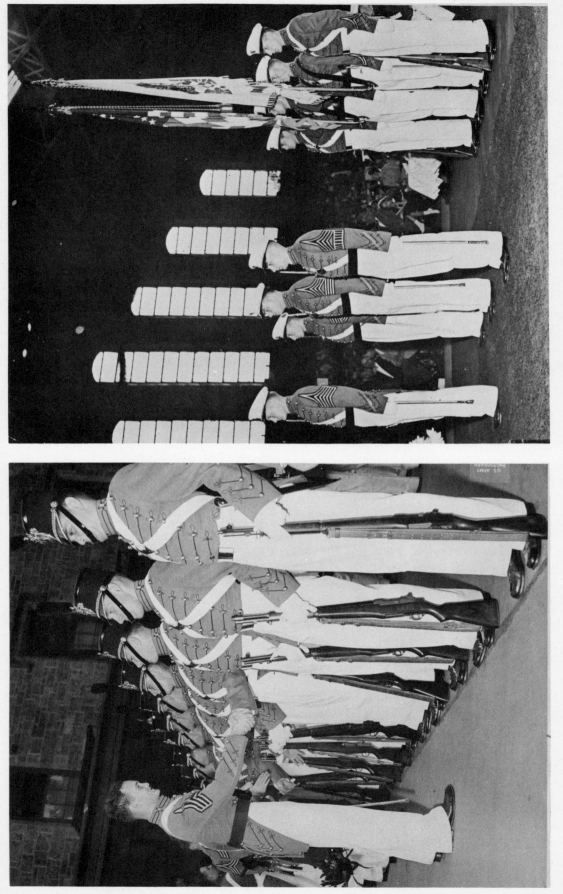

These are "The Wheels" at the Graduation exercises: the First Captain (Corps Commander), his staff (Adjutant, Supply Officer, and Training Officer), followed by the Corps Colors (carried on this special occasion by Second Classmen, corporals not yet assigned to this duty). All are wearing the June Week uniform. Cadet officers are appointed on the basis of merit.

In a special Recognition Ceremony during June Week, the Plebes are "recognized" by the upperclassmen for the first time as members of the Corps. Here we can see the Plebes "brace" themselves at rigid attention for the last time, as the First Classmen, with plumed hats under their arms, march down the lines to shake their hands.

What Cadet Gray Means

We have said that the Corps has its own special uniform. To be more exact, the Corps has several special uniforms. Some are more distinctive than others, but in one way or another they differ from uniforms worn by anyone else. There are uniforms prescribed for use in classrooms, others for parade, still others for athletics, and so on. There are winter uniforms and others for summer; a long overcoat for cold days, a jacket for cool days, a raincoat for rainy days, and rough field clothing for maneuvers. There are sixteen authorized types of military dress, but this does not count the athletic nor the bad weather clothing.

Every West Point cadet is an ambassador of good will for the Academy, and his cadet gray uniform is immediately recognized as belonging to West Point. A cadet's pride in the Corps is evident in the way he walks, talks, and conducts himself. He is proud to have won his appointment to this greatest of Academies, and the fact that he has had to work hard to maintain his position adds to his pride of achievement. To him and to the general public a cadet gray uniform is the symbol of a fine all-round man.

The story of the wearing of cadet gray is much more than the story of ordinary clothes or ordinary uniforms; in fact, more than the story of Army uniforms in general. In the cadet's life the uniform plays a role unheard of by the ordinary soldier. The painstaking attention the cadet gives his uniform is best illustrated by a story of the white trousers which have been worn at West Point since the earliest days. This is what a member of the Class of 1923 recalled and wrote thirty years later, about his white trousers:

"Eight pairs, as I remember, were issued about the time we went to camp. They were of white duck. Since we wore them constantly during the summer, except at weekday reveille, breakfast, and drill, and when it was raining, and since laundry was sent and received only twice a week, good organization was required to have the white trousers always in good condition. The usual procedure was to put on a fresh pair for parade and then to wear that pair for successive formations in the following order: Chapel, noon meal formation, supper formation, other formations. This meant that we usually had two or three used pairs in our tents 'marked' for different formations.

"A calamity occurred shortly after our arrival in camp as plebes. The much-respected Commandant died and the Corps was turned out in full dress with raincoats for the funeral ceremonies. Since the plebes did not have uniform gray trousers to wear with full dress coats, all cadets were ordered to

Lieut. General Blackshear M. Bryan, Superintendent, U.S.M.A.

New cadets arriving at West Point are greeted by members of the "New Cadet Detail." The first thing they learn is how to "brace" and take orders. The upperclassmen greet them in the traditional Dress Gray over white. This picture was taken in the Central Area in 1918.

In the same Area, the Corps stands inspection by the Superintendent of the Korean Military Academy in January, 1953. The cadets in the foreground are officers, as indicated by their chevrons, swords and sashes.

wear white trousers. The rain not only left the trousers thoroughly bedraggled and unfit for use before another laundering, but the Cadet Laundry was unable for some months to remove completely the mud stains from the trousers.

"Cadets at that time took extraordinary precautions to keep from wrinkling their trousers. Ordinarily, to put them on, we carefully turned the waists down over the legs as far as the crotch, climbed up on a chair, and carefully put in one leg at a time while depressing the toes to the limit; then the waists were carefully turned up. Cadets going to meet special visitors or attending a hop would frequently swing from the alcove partition while their roommates would put their trousers on them. It was then customary to walk stiff-legged, at least until the camp or barracks area had been cleared. We always carefully creased the trousers back of the knee and near the shoe top before putting them on to insure that they would 'break' in the proper place instead of sagging generally. In the Mess Hall all cadets, upperclassmen and plebes alike, sat well forward on the front edge of their chairs and with their feet stuck out in front to keep from getting avoidable wrinkles in their trousers. All of this was a matter of pride and not of regulation. Automobiles were then 'off limits' and we never even considered submitting our precious trousers to the pernicious treatment now taken as a matter of course in the Corps.

"Another matter of concern with regard to all trousers was to adjust them so that the backs came down to the tops of our heels. We felt undressed if they were any higher.

"When a class graduated there was a great rush to 'inherit' white trousers from members of the outgoing class. Lucky was the cadet who acquired in this way half a dozen extra pairs of trousers. In my time some pairs of *linen* trousers of a remote period had been handed down for many years. They were slightly less white than the duck trousers but they had the great advantage of wrinkling less and of straightening out more readily if they were hung up after wearing.

"The first of June was traditionally the day for beginning the wearing of white trousers. If I remember correctly, they were first worn to reveille that day, although during the rest of the summer

A cadet dressing for parade cannot compromise with the angle of his pompon or the fit of his belt. Every detail of his dress must be exact. His hat must be *exactly* centered on his head and *exactly* straight.

gray trousers were uniform for that occasion. White trousers were also worn to classes during the three or four days of academic work remaining of June, for June Week generally started the second week in that month. We also wore white trousers to classes in the fall until the middle of September."

Such an account makes one realize that the Corps of Cadets has no superior in the world for perfect dress. Only a few outfits such as the Brigade of Guards in England or the French Foreign Legion can approach it for flawless drill, iron discipline and unbreakable tradition.

The Military Academy is like any other academy or college in that it educates men in how to think straight and how to study profitably and how, in general, to face the world ahead with confidence. But it has another job; it must teach a cadet how to command other men in battle — a great responsibility. The safety as well as effectiveness of all the soldiers he leads through the hazards of war depends largely on how well the officer knows his

"Walking the Area" is a way cadets who have disobeyed regulations may wipe out their demerits. In this drawing by R. F. Zogbaum, made in 1886, the Area Birds are wearing "forage" caps. Except for the caps and arrangement of belts, this is the uniform seen in winter today.

business.

Among the first lessons a cadet must learn is the meaning of discipline — how to accept and carry out orders of a superior, cheerfully and thoroughly. No man is fit to give orders who has not first learned to take them. The strict obedience of the many regulations in force at the Military Academy is part of its training in discipline. Cadets who have disobeyed regulations are given demerits, some of which may be "walked off" by marching back and forth in the barracks yard for specific periods of time. The picture on this page shows "Area Birds" engaged in "walking the area," a sight as common now as in 1886.

About 1840 several important changes were made in accouterments. Among other things the cadet was given a little black percussion box to be worn on the waist belt exactly "one inch from the right edge of the waist plate."

Precise placement has always governed everything a cadet has and does. His full dress hat must be *exactly* centered on his head and *exactly* straight, its pompon must extend forward from the vertical *exactly* 30 degrees. Back in 1845, therefore, we are not surprised to hear that the upper edge of the cartridge box was to "be three inches below the lower edge of the waist belt," or that on 31 August,

1847, orders were issued to increase this distance to four inches. Such precision in details, distressful as it may seem to some people, teaches a cadet a sense of orderliness and exact thinking he never forgets. An army that lacks these two characteristics is an army beaten before it has started to fight.

The Corps has its own special language, its numerous traditions, its strict code of personal honor, and its rigid discipline, but it also has its standing jokes. A new cadet does not gain full "recognition" as a member of the Corps until the end of his first year. In fact, this recognition takes place significantly in a special ceremony in June. Until then he is a "Plebe" (from the Roman word for a member of the lowest class). Should he presume on his position by showing a lack of respect for upperclassmen, he is treated for "B.J.," or "Bold before June," in no uncertain terms.

The First Uniform

Since the first cadets at West Point had belonged to the Artillerists and Engineers, they wore its uniform: a dark blue cutaway coat with scarlet "facings," brass buttons, white or blue waistcoat and tight pantaloons, black leather boots, a large cocked hat with a black cockade and a scarlet feather plume. Every detail of this uniform meant something very real to its wearers, and they saw to it that other troops did not encroach upon the same "regimentals."

It must be remembered that the Artillerists and the Engineers of this period were a cut above other soldiers. The officers, in particular, had to be educated men, who knew something of mathematics, chemistry, mechanics and the other elements of Natural Philosophy. They were technicians as well as soldiers. Perhaps the Cavalrymen cut more dashing figures — perhaps they were wealthier and better born — but the Artillerists and the Engineers were military scholars who took their trade and the science of war seriously. Our Chief of Artillery in the Revolution had been Henry Knox, formerly a bookseller and an avid student of tactics. Pierre L'Enfant, who later laid out the City of Washington, and Thaddeus Kosciuszko, the celebrated Polish patriot, were Engineer officers in that war and authors of books on military subjects. Later Artillerists and Engineers like Louis de Tousard and Jonathan Williams were no less scholarly, and Williams founded our first service association for the theoretical study of military science. Just then

A private (matross) of the Regiment of Artillerists and Engineers which garrisoned West Point in 1795. He is attired here in winter dress. Over his "round hat" runs a wide strip of bearskin; his uniform is blue with scarlet facings, and his buttons are of brass. Drawing by H. Charles McBarron, Jr.

one of their brotherhood — a French Artillery officer named Napoleon Bonaparte — was making a great name for himself in Europe.

All over the world Artillerists wore dark blue coats, trimmed with red, almost as if it were an international uniform. Their buttons were brass and their braid was of gold lace — "yellow metal" to distinguish them from Infantrymen who had to wear "white metal" buttons of pewter or (for officers) silver. In the American service this important distinction lasted until 1851, and was not abolished without protest.

The cadets of the Artillerists and Engineers were dressed like the junior officers of the Regiments but with blue shoulder straps edged with gold lace instead of epaulettes, or perhaps with one epaulette on the left shoulder. Cadets wore brass mounted swords (for swords then, and for years afterwards, were the most important symbol of the officer) suspended from white leather shoulder belts. However, they were not allowed to tie on sword knots; these came after graduation, when they had been commissioned as officers.

Tomb of the Polish-American patriot, Kosciuszko, at West Point, as seen in an 1837 drawing by Professor W. H. Bartlett. Note that the cadet is wearing sherrivallies, which button up the side of his legs all the way from heel to hip, a style popular at the time. On his head is a "bell-crowned cap" made of leather.

After 1802 their buttons carried the eagle and cannon insignia of the Regiment of Artillerists, one of the first regimental insignia to be adopted in the United States. We have also mentioned the cockade; it was the sign of the soldier in those days. Regulations for the Artillerists ordered that the soldier wear one "in all Situations, as an honorable distinction and badge of his profession, and as acknowledgment that he receives the pay and is in the Service of the United States."

Often the cadets at West Point drilled with muskets; these were flintlock weapons, .69 caliber, which were being manufactured in America. The regulation musket was 5 feet in length and weighed about 8½ pounds — quite a load for a boy in his early teens. For the younger cadets, therefore, a few smaller French "musketoons" were procured

Cadets about 1802 probably carried swords like this French grenadier model. Sergeants in the Revolutionary Army had previously carried them. The hilt is all brass.

in June, 1802. They were never popular, however, for no cadet was willing to admit being weaker than the rest.

In this uniform and with this equipage the cadets drilled and studied, up to about 1810. It was almost the same dress in which their fathers had fought through the Revolution — comfortable and serviceable — not too different from the dress of the civilian except for its uniform color, and its facings, and the cockade that distinguished him as a soldier.

Cadet in winter uniform, 1802. The drawing suggests he is a junior officer, judging by his sword, boots, crimson sash, white belt and single epaulette, but the absence of a sword knot indicates he is a cadet. The drawing is by Colonel Harry C. Larter, Jr.

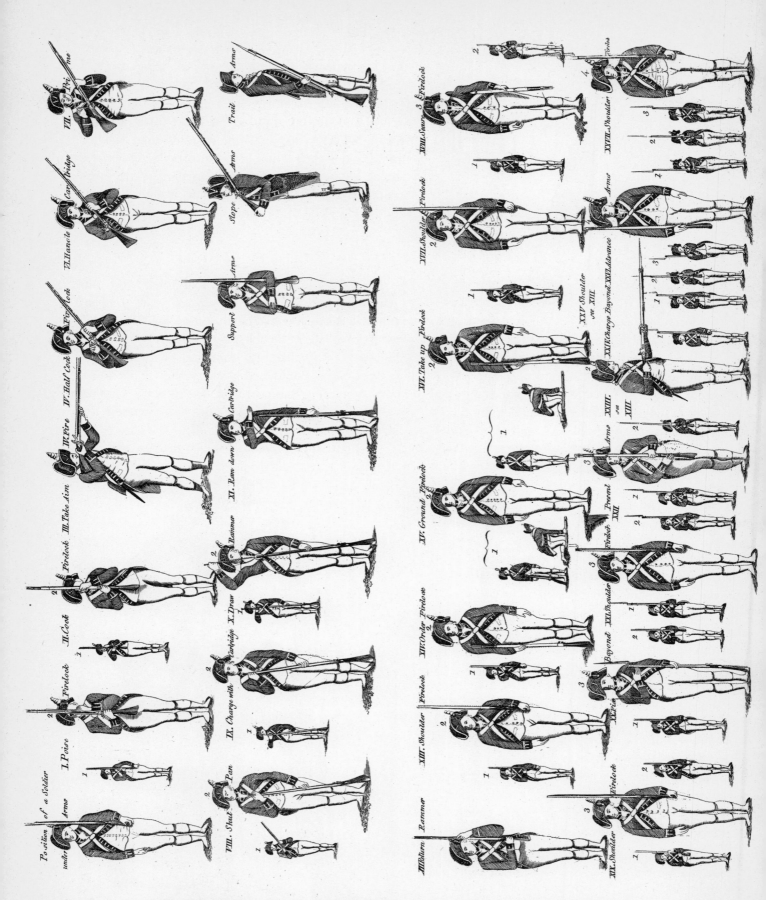

The "Manual Exercise" for Infantry in 1802, from an edition of Steuben's *Regulations*, published in Boston. This remained the official manual at West Point until about 1812.

Republican Styles

In a preceding chapter we have seen how, in spite of a bill signed by President Thomas Jefferson on 16 March 1802, it was not for ten years or so that a full-fledged military school was established. During these lean years, quarters and classrooms were inadequate, instructors few and not always competent, and textbooks almost non-existent. Cadets slept on the floor, studied by candlelight in bare rooms heated by small wood fires, and ate a monotonous diet of meat, potatoes and bread. Usually, only a handful of the cadets could be mustered for classes.

Yet there was at least one significant development during these years. West Point in this period became a school for the Army as a whole; its students were given a uniform that marked them solely as cadets. We cannot be entirely certain when this event took place; there were so few boys at West Point that it did not seem worthwhile to write elaborate regulations on how they should dress. Probably the change in uniforms was a gradual development, which, by 1810, seems to have been completely effected. No longer did cadets wear the uniform of Artillery, or Engineers, or some other branch of the service.

The new uniform was not significantly distinctive of West Point alone — it also reflected a change in dress taking place all over Europe and America, for at this time there was a revolutionary change in people's outlook and way of living, clearly reflected in the way they dressed.

The first Superintendent of the U.S.M.A., from 1802 to 1812, Colonel Jonathan Williams, as seen in a portrait by Thomas Sully which now hangs in the West Point Library. He is dressed in blue and is wearing gilt Engineer Corps buttons. Castle Williams on Governors Island in New York Harbor, which he built, is in the background of the painting.

From 1775 to 1783, we had fought for our American Independence. Within ten years the people of France revolted against the "Old Regime," as they called it — the royalty and nobility who had held sway there for centuries. They not only tried to wipe out the aristocracy, but to do away with everything that stood for the old days. Clothes — always before their eyes — were among the first things to be changed.

For a century or more men of fashion and soldiers had worn cocked hats, cutaway coats, buckled shoes, and knee breeches. They had kept their long hair braided and powdered! The French revolu-

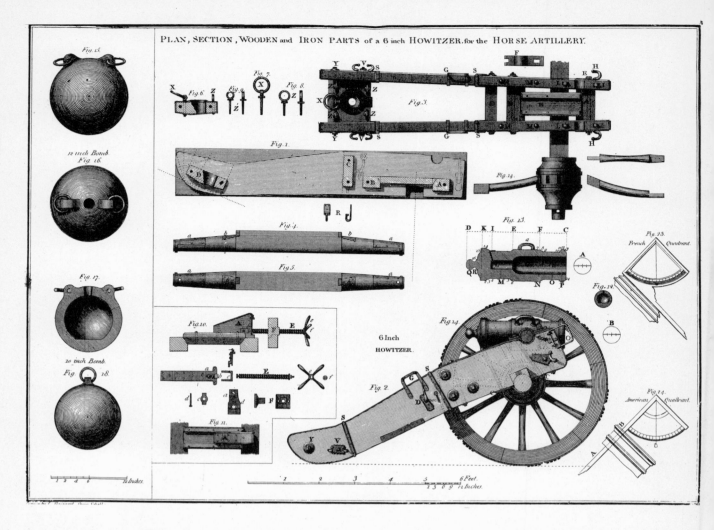

PLAN, SECTION, WOODEN and IRON PARTS of a 6 inch HOWITZER for the HORSE ARTILLERY.

Field (or Horse) Artillery of the early Nineteenth Century. This plate is from Louis de Tousard's *American Artillerist's Companion* of 1809, which was used as a text at the Military Academy.

tionists obliterated these symbols of aristocracy — in America those citizens who sympathized with them followed suit. President Jefferson was a leader in this movement, and scarcely two months after he took office in 1801, the Army uniform began to change.

First went the long powdered hair; soldiers' heads were ordered to be "cropped." Then the "round hat" was introduced — it resembled somewhat the present-day high hat. The President personally introduced long trousers (called "pantaloons"), and high, buttoned shoes. Though many officers were shocked by these innovations the enlisted men, on the whole, welcomed them.

An event occurred in 1807 that gave these changes special importance. On 22 June a partially armed U.S. frigate, the *Chesapeake,* was fired upon

and boarded by the British frigate *Leopard,* off Hampton Roads. The attack, following on the heels of a series of like annoyances, roused new and violent anti-British feeling which led Congress, the following year, to more than double the Regular Army. When the time came to clothe and accouter this new force, the uniform selected was of the radically new style in almost every detail.

By 1810, the cadets at West Point had received this new dress. For fatigue wear they wore round hats. However, cocked hats (now called "chapeaux de bras" because they could be folded flat and carried under the arm) were retained for formal occasions and probably for parade. Coats were cut straight across the waist and buttoned down the front. For daily use their tails were short (these were called "coatees"), while other coats with longer tails were worn for full dress. Fairly tight pantaloons reached down to the ankles. All the scarlet trimmings were gone; indeed, the cadet uniform of those years was severely plain. The dark

U.S.M.A. CADETS IN WINTER DRESS, ABOUT 1812

After a permanent Military Academy was established in 1802, cadets like these were given a distinctive uniform of their own.

The "round hat" similar to the popular civilian hat of the times, was worn for classes and fatigue duty.

blue coatee was relieved only by "false button-holes" of narrow black braid. Probably by 1814 they had brass "bullet" buttons, about which we will see more later.

In 1807 the Government commenced to manufacture some short muskets, or carbines, of .54 caliber to be given to friendly Indians in the West. A cry of protest from frontiersmen ended the plan, and in 1813 a few were sent to West Point for the younger cadets. Again, the little guns were disliked and rarely used.

When drilling with muskets, cadets wore white cross belts, fastened in front by a brass plate, from which hung a black leather cartridge box and a bayonet scabbard. White belts have ever since been worn at West Point for dress parade. Regulations called for a brass-mounted sword to be carried at other times, but not all cadets owned one and some preferred a small dirk. Variations of this sort in dress and fatigue uniform were quite common in those days. Indeed, one cadet who graduated in 1820, recalled that "everything [was] worn, according to fancy, up to a major-general's uniform."

Officer of the Regiment of Artillerists, about 1807. Companies of this Regiment were stationed at West Point until 1812. This officer is attired in an old-fashioned cutaway coat and wears a "chapeau de bras," so called because this cocked hat could be folded flat and carried under the arm. This painting is by H. Charles McBarron, Jr.

Partridge's Gray Uniform

When, in 1812, the United States, for a second time, went to war with Great Britain, the West Point cadets who were ready hastened off to join the Army. The war lasted not one year, but almost three. Although, in the end, we managed to win, it was only after suffering a series of bitter defeats. The worst, of course, was the capture and burning of our new capital at Washington, D. C. In this war, the first West Pointer died in battle. He was 28-year old Ensign George Ronan, Class of 1811, killed in a hand-to-hand fight with the British and Indians at Fort Chicago, the site of the present city of that name.

In the midst of the war the Army's supply of blue cloth ran out. This — the color worn by most of the soldiers — had been dyed with indigo, imported from abroad. As substitutes, the Army bought up cloth of any kind and color it could lay its hands on, the most common being a rough gray cloth of the sort used for work clothing. Apparently, fatigue uniforms made of this material were sent to West Point in the summer of 1814.

A shipment of these same gray uniforms went to Buffalo, New York, where Brigadier General Winfield Scott was drilling his 1st Brigade of Regular Infantry. The men at first were disgusted at having to wear the gray cloth, for it was the clothing worn by Negro slaves and also by some of the poorer volunteer companies who had proved to be cowards in the earlier battles with the British.

But Winfield Scott was an able and firm instructor, and he didn't give his soldiers much time to worry about their clothes. During the spring of 1814, he whipped them into a crack outfit, resolute and proud. On the Fourth of July, at their head he marched out to meet the British near the Chippewa River in Canada. Because of what happened there, the cadets wear gray at West Point, today.

Scott's four Regular regiments, dressed in the gray uniform of the volunteers, formed in a wide line of battle. Far out ahead of them stood the British battalions, their heavy 24-pounders loaded. At a roll of the drums the gray line started forward, as steady as on parade, their great blue and buff regimental colors flowing above rows of shiny black caps. The British gunners waited until the Americans were within 600 yards, then lowered their lighted linstocks to the touch holes of the cannon.

Major-General Riall, the British commander, sat on horseback, and watched the gray ranks come

J. R. Bartlett Del.   A. Willard Sc.

The man responsible for cadets' wearing gray was Captain Alden Partridge, Superintendent of the Academy from 1815 to 1817. The cadets called him "Old Pewter," possibly because his own uniform and those he ordered manufactured for the cadets were gray. This drawing of Captain Partridge by J. B. Bartlett was published in J. Holbrook's *Military Tactics* of 1826.

This 1814 battle at Chippewa led to the adoption of the gray uniform at West Point. The courageous charge of General Winfield Scott's Regulars in gray coats aroused Partridge's admiration. Painting by H. Charles McBarron, Jr.

closer. He was not worried for he had whipped militiamen in gray uniforms before. But as he watched his round shot rip great holes through the American line and saw it still come steadily on, he realized his mistake.

"Those are Regulars, by God!" he cried, and a few minutes later Scott's men swarmed over his position and captured his guns. The gray brigade had not merely won a battle; after seemingly endless failures, it had restored the American soldiers' faith in themselves.

Captain Alden Partridge was Superintendent of the Military Academy at the time. Looking for ways to raise West Point's efficiency in the confusion of war time, he realized that gray had become a badge of honor. He had a uniform made of this color for himself and wore it at every opportunity. The cadets called him "Old Pewter," possibly because of the gray color of his clothing. More important still, he had orders placed with John B. Thorp, a New York tailor, for new cadet uniforms of gray

satinette, a cloth of good quality. These arrived in the summer of 1815.

Partridge also ordered smart leather caps with plumes and brass plates, much like those worn by Scott's men at Chippewa. The new uniforms were far more military-looking than the old blues. Down the front ran three rows of buttons connected by double rows of black braid, arranged in a herringbone pattern, with "Austrian knots" at their ends. Braid also adorned the collar, cuffs, swallowtails and the front of the gray winter pantaloons. White pantaloons, buttoned all the way down the side and called "sherrivallies," were worn for a time in the summer months. It was, in fact, very similar to the uniform the cadets wear today.

The big brass cap plate adopted by Partridge for the cadets was almost the same as that worn by the

The National Color of the 11th U.S. Infantry, 1812-1814, one of the regiments that charged with Scott's Brigade at Chippewa.

The brass cap plate adopted by Partridge, 1815-1816, is the earliest known insignia of the U.S.M.A. It was almost the same as that worn by Scott's Regulars. (Note that the engraver hardly left enough room for the "Y" of Academy.) This plate was not discovered until 1954, and previously no one knew what it looked like. Owned by Waverly P. Lewis, Devon, Conn.

Regulars, except that the words "MILITARY ACADEMY" were stamped across the top. He must have had the work done by a local artisan who had a hard time fitting in the last letter.

The buttons on the new uniform are of particular interest. They were "bullet," "ball," or "bell" buttons, so-called because they were shaped like the round lead bullet of that day, or like small round sleigh bells. This style of button was new in our Army though it was beginning to be worn by officers of the Corps of Engineers and others on the staff. Partridge may have adopted it to show the close connection of the Military Academy with the Engineers. But it seems more likely that because bullet buttons are round, they sparkle far more than do the flat kind, and we can be quite certain that sparkle was what the Superintendent wanted.

SUPERINTENDENT PARTRIDGE AND CADETS, U.S.M.A., SUMMER PARADE DRESS, ABOUT 1815

These cadets wore a big brass plate on the leather caps with the words "Military Academy" stamped across the top. When drilling with muskets the cadets wore a brass plate to fasten their white cross belts in front. The Superintendent wears a "chapeau de bras," which folded, and could be carried under his arm.

Cadet Dress in Thayer's Time

In 1816 the Secretary of War formally approved the use of gray uniforms for the Military Academy, and the color has not changed since. The coatee was, and still is, the then popular "swallowtail" or "claw-hammer" style. For reasons of economy, the War Department abolished the leather cap introduced by Captain Partridge and ordered cadets back into the "common round hat" worn by civilians.

Gray and black, relieved by sparkling brass and white — and here and there by the crimson of a sash — became the traditional colors of West Point. The spreading fame of the Military Academy eventually led other American military schools, as they were formed, to adopt much the same dress.

In 1817, Major Sylvanus Thayer of the Corps of Engineers became Superintendent at West Point. A fine teacher, a remarkable administrator, as Superintendent he was able to foresee and plan for the great future of the institution. His statue, which stands on the Plain, has this inscription on its pedestal: "Father of the Military Academy."

Many of the academic principles and systems now used at the Military Academy date from Thayer's period. He was the first to issue a diploma to every cadet who graduated — a tangible proof of four years of hard work and good conduct. This was first given out about 1823, and on it was engraved

The Corps at artillery drill on the Plain in 1828. The cadet cannoneers are wearing forage caps. The cadet in the foreground has wide pantaloons strapped under his instep, a style typical of the 1820's. He and the ladies were not in the original painting by George Catlin, but added by J. Hill, when he engraved it.

the picture you see here: a cadet in the "bell-crowned" leather cap adopted some years before (about 1818).

This cap was a majestic, if ungainly, headdress with a diamond-shaped brass plate, chin strap, and gold lace cords. It was called "bell-crowned" because, when turned upside down, its top looked like the mouth of an old-fashioned bell. To the front of the cap was fixed an eight-inch black feather pompon, much the same distinctive decoration as the cadets wear today.

With its trimmings, the cap cost over $8, a great expense for the cadet who had to buy one out of his meager allowance of $16 a month. It was also uncomfortable. One cadet, who had not learned the mysteries of fitting it to his head, wrote feelingly to his mother: "The skin is coming off my face up to my nose on account of standing Guard yesterday

for four hours during the most intense heat, and we are obliged to wear those tall bell-crowned leather Caps which with the brass trimmings weigh about 5 Pounds and hurt my head extremely and the rim also coming just to the nose." Nevertheless the bell-crowned cap was worn at West Point until 1839.

We have spoken several times of white pantaloons. Made of linen or of a lightweight cotton, such as jean or "Russia sheeting," these were widely worn in summer by all American troops including West Point cadets. The earlier pantaloons had been quite tight. Then, about 1815, "sherrivallies," buttoned up the side, became popular. During the first

Part of the embellishment of the U.S.M.A. diploma, introduced about 1823 and, with some changes, used today. The artist for this diploma rendered the details of the uniform crudely, and omitted the cross belts which are always worn when the musket is carried.

(Above) Major Sylvanus Thayer is probably the man on the right in this picture of three officers at West Point, as painted by George Catlin about 1827. Note the "chapeaux de bras."

(Below) How an infantry drill would be performed about 1826. Note the bell-crowned caps and wide pantaloons. This drawing is from J. Holbrook's *Military Tactics*.

(Above) A fine example of the leather cockade of this period at West Point. The cockade was the mark of the military man and was worn as late as the 1850's.

years of Thayer's regime, cadets had worn loose "Cossack" pantaloons, popularized by the Russians garrisoning Paris in 1815-1818. The Board of Visitors complained in 1820 that the pantaloons had

This beautifully decorated sword was worn by Major Thayer at West Point. Note the insignia of the Corps of Engineers — a castle, eagle and rising sun — on the counter-guard. This was the same device that Engineer officers of the period wore on their buttons.

WEST POINT CADETS IN SUMMER DRESS AND FATIGUE CLOTHING, 1835

The cadet with the stick is in cotton fatigues, with a soft leather forage cap. The others are in dress uniforms with "bell-crowned" caps. The cadet officer in the background wears a sash and gold cords on his cap.

(Above) The U.S. Military Academy as seen from the ferry landing and railroad station at Garrisons, across the river from West Point about 1840. Note the steam ferry in the dock and the cords of wood piled high on shore.

A leather forage cap is worn by the cadet sitting here on Trophy Point, reading to his lady. A Professor of Drawing at the Academy, Robert W. Weir, made the original painting from which James Smillie made this engraving in 1836.

been so shortened "in compliance with the present fashion, so as to leave an unsightly gap between them and the uniform shoe." As a result, the pantaloons were lengthened and strapped under the instep.

When we see the trouble to which the modern cadet must go to keep his starched Whites spotless and sharply pressed, it seems queer that soldiers once wore white cotton trousers all day long, even on campaign. But in those days the pantaloons were never starched nor pressed, for pressing is a recent fashion, dating from about 1890. Above all, cotton pants could be readily washed by the soldier, and he could not wash wool. Stains could be covered by the same pipe-clay used for the white leather belts (much as modern cadets use chalk they get from the blackboards).

Until the 1870's (when the breech-loading rifle was generally adopted) infantrymen had to do most of their fighting standing erect, for it was very hard to load a muzzle-loading musket while lying down. There was no hugging the dirt for cover in those

Cadets relaxing around the Cadet Monument about 1822. Being off duty, the cadets wear only swords, though one of them has on a shoulder belt. This water color was possibly painted by J. R. Smith, Class of 1823.

days, or crouching in muddy trenches, as the soldier does now. Thus it was possible for a soldier to keep his uniform in a fairly clean state, and to wear a pair of white trousers several days in a row.

Another very distinctive part of the cadet uniform originated in this period. Before Major Thayer's time the degree of rank of a commissioned or non-commissioned officer in the Army had been indicated primarily by the kind of epaulette he wore on his shoulders. The Corps was now large enough to require a number of cadet officers, and in 1817 the Superintendent ordered that their rank be indicated by means of chevrons worn on the sleeve. For some years, European armies had been using strips of cloth sewn on the arm to distinguish sergeants and corporals, and Thayer probably got the idea from them. He applied it to cadet officers of all grades.

The two chevrons pointing down on this cadet's right arm indicate that he was a cadet lieutenant. The picture is of Washington Wheelwright, Class of 1821, and the painting was made in oil on wood by an unknown artist. It is now in the U.S.M.A. Library.

This first system was unsatisfactory and a new one was devised the following year. The second was rather complicated, since some chevrons pointed up and others down, and it made a difference on which arm they were worn, but it remained in effect until the present system was prescribed in 1830.

It is interesting to note that the Army adopted the chevron method of showing rank a few years after Thayer instituted it, applying it to all uniforms up to and including captains. In 1830 chevrons were abolished for commissioned officers, but on the arms of sergeants and corporals they remained to become one of the proudest symbols in the Army. When, during the Second World War, chevrons were authorized for technicians and others who had not yet learned real soldiering, the chevron lost much distinction. In 1955, at last, the Army reserved the chevron for the arms of the real non-commissioned officer.

Nowhere in the Army today except in the Corps of Cadets can one find the chevron still used to denote captains and lieutenants.

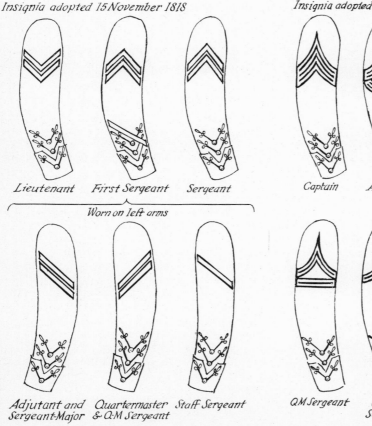

Insignia adopted 15 November 1818

Captain   Lieutenant   First Sergeant   Sergeant

Worn on left arms

Corporal   Adjutant and Sergeant-Major   Quartermaster & Q·M Sergeant   Staff Sergeant

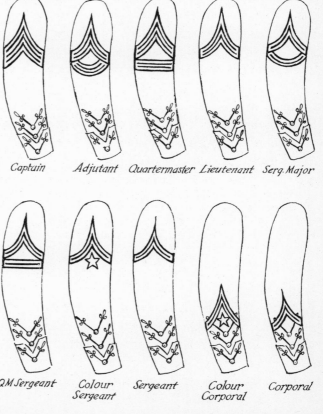

Insignia adopted 29 June 1830. All chevrons are worn on both arms

Captain   Adjutant   Quartermaster   Lieutenant   Serg. Major

QM Sergeant   Colour Sergeant   Sergeant   Colour Corporal   Corporal

The West Point Band

Since the first forts were built, West Point has echoed to martial music. Before the Military Academy was founded, the fifes and drums of the Regiment of Artillerists and Engineers played the marches and calls needed by the garrison. The first cadets must have listened to many of the same tunes their descendants do now, when, at noon each day, the fifes and drums of the "Hell Cats" play them into mess.

The first true band to play for the Corps of Cadets was formed in 1813 from the band of the 3rd U.S. Artillery, which was transferred to West Point from Governor's Island for the purpose. The members seem to have been able musicians, and their drum major, who came from Litchfield, Connecticut, bore the name of George Washington.

In April 1815, Superintendent Partridge, as part of his attempt to boost the spirit at the Academy, requisitioned for these musicians twenty red coats, trimmed with black and yellow. His selection of red was not unusual; it was the color worn by most American bandsmen of those days.

Basically, the red coat stemmed from the principle of "reverse colors," by which the trumpeters or drummers of a regiment were commonly dressed in a combination of colors which were the reverse of the rest of the soldiers. This enabled a commander readily to pick out a musician (who was his principal means of signalling) in the dense smoke of battle, to have him blow or beat a call.

In the Revolution, many of our regiments had worn red trimmings ("facings") on their varied colored coats; and their drummers, by tradition, had been put in red coats. The scarlet coats, captured from the British, were appropriated for this use. So the practice started, and for years Army Regulations ordered that "coatees of musicians will be of scarlet cloth." Today the U.S. Marine Band still dresses in red.

The red coat was worn by the West Point Band until 1820. Unhappily, this was also the color of the uniform of the fifers and drummers of the Company of Bombardiers, Sappers and Miners — the Engineer Corps unit then stationed at West Point. The serious musicians of the Band resented being confused with mere field music (as fifes and drums were called) and pleaded for a different uniform. After much effort, Major Thayer got them an entirely new outfit in 1820, consisting of white coats with red trimmings.

This white and red uniform proved popular. The Band, still consisting of twenty musicians, wore it until 1832 when the style was modified but the colors continued. Field music — six fifers and six drummers — was added in 1841. White was the dress uniform until War Department orders in 1850 changed it to a dark blue frock coat trimmed with red on collar and cuffs. With some variation, this more somber uniform was worn throughout the Civil War period.

The Civil War over, the Band returned to its old white and red. Deliberately the "cadet pattern" tailcoat was revived and from 1867 to 1873 the musicians at West Point rivalled in gayety of dress any circus band that ever led elephants down the street.

The military bands of these early years would sound strange and discordant to our ears today. Their wind instruments were crudely constructed and difficult to keep in tune, and for the most part, were without valves for changing key. On the other hand, skill in drumming was at its peak in the early 1800's.

WEST POINT BAND, 1818

Skill in drumming was at its peak in the early 1800's. The drum major, with baton, sword and baldric, is a most colorful and impressive figure as he leads his twenty musicians.

(Right) Trumpeter and drummer of the Field Music at the Barracks sally-port, waiting to play a call. This is an old picture of what the cadets call the "Hell Cats." (Below) The West Point band during the Civil War attired in army regulation headdress (sometimes called the "Jeff Davis" hat) with frock coats and trousers of dark blue.

We would also be surprised at the slow, stately march steps at which the Band led the cadets on parade. The Common Time for marching in 1813, for example, was 75 steps a minute, whereas the Quickest Time was 120 steps. Today, cadets regularly march at 124 steps a minute, a pace considered to be in keeping with smartness and élan of modern times. Yet anyone who has observed the French Foreign Legion on parade knows how impressive the old "slow-march" can be.

No part of a military unit is so laden with tradition as its band. For one thing, it must be colorfully dressed; and its drum major, out in front, must be the most colorful and impressive of all. This springs from his origin centuries ago as a "whiffler," or one who marched before a ruler and prepared the way.

White dress uniform was worn by the West Point Band, 1867-1873. Its trimmings were red. The jackets worn by the two field musicians were also red.

Sometimes the whifflers brandished immense swords (a custom fortunately abandoned) and at other times they wielded batons, from which the present day drum major's baton derives.

The drum major once had several duties beside leading the band. He was supposed to train the drummers, to distribute the mail and, in some regiments, to act as a banker for the other soldiers. His badges of office were his baton, his distinctive hat (often of bearskin), and his baldric, or wide shoulder belts. On the baldric was almost always to be found a pair of miniature drumsticks. The drum major of the West Point Band wears the ceremonial baldric and sticks today.

Since 1870 the West Point band has increased in size from about 32 bandsmen and 12 field musicians to 92 and 47, respectively; and the Director, a lieutenant colonel, is now assisted by three other officers. The Field Music, during this interval, earned its name of "Hell Cats" from the cadets, who are awakened each morning by squeals and flams of its fifes and drums.

About 1875, the Band changed its white and red uniforms for new ones of dark blue. Since then it has stuck to this color for dress and full dress. By 1892, it was wearing spiked helmets for full dress, and sometimes horsehair plumes that waved in the breeze. Throughout this period the drum major continued to sport his heavy bearskin hat and his baldric with the miniature drumsticks.

In 1857 a British officer wrote about the Band: "The drum-major was 'got up' with a bear skin, in the French style, and the band were distinguished by broad yellow lapels to their blue frocks." These were the men he saw.

(Above) The West Point Band about 1880 was dressed in blue. The change in uniform color was made in 1873 and it has remained blue ever since.

(Below) In common with most of the Army, the Band wore spiked helmets in the 1890's. These helmets were adopted after the Prussians had won the Franco-Prussian War in 1871.

(Above) The Band leads the parade, with the Corps following, in a picture about 1905 in Washington, D. C. The parade is coming down Pennsylvania Avenue toward the White House and the Capitol can be seen dimly in the distance.

(Below) By 1912, the drum major's bearskin hat has gone. This picture of the Band in formation on Trophy Point shows the summer Full Dress uniform, almost the same as is worn by the Band today.

A retiring general shakes hands with the Director of the West Point Band, 1954. The Director and other officers, in summer dress uniform, carry swords and the drum major is wearing his wide belt known as a baldric.

Soon after the Corps adopted the new tarbucket hat in 1899 the Band did likewise, and it wears this hat now for full dress. It uses regulation khaki for drill in summer and the Army dress blues in winter. Its officers still wear swords on parade.

A closeup of the drum major in winter Full Dress uniform, showing his baldric with the pair of miniature drumsticks. His headdress is the cadet Full Dress cap but with white cords and plume, and a special device.

Plumes, Swords and Other Distinctions

In 1839 the cadets were issued a new dress cap — a straight-sided affair "shaped like a section of stovepipe." It was made of black beaver, with leather bands around its top and bottom. Above the crown stood a black worsted pompon, eight inches long, set in a yellow metal socket. To its front was fastened a brass eagle and crossed cannon. It was, in fact, the same cap as worn by the Regular Artillery, except for the pompon.

Major Delafield of the Corps of Engineers, Superintendent at the time, was upset about this use of the Artillery insignia. He wrote the Chief of Engineers urging that the castle (the insignia of Engineers) be worn instead. In those days, it must be remembered, West Point was run by Engineers, although only a few of its highest ranking graduates actually entered that Corps. Indeed, until 1835, West Point was the only engineering school in the United States, and up to the Civil War was the leading school of its kind. At a time when the expansion of the United States required engineers, this was a vital contribution to the nation, and the largest part of the Western exploration — surveying, and railroad construction — fell to West Pointers.

In 1839, however, there was no Engineer cap insignia being made, for there were no Engineer soldiers — only officers who wore other sorts of headdress. But Major Delafield persevered, and in 1842 a small supply of brass castles was received at West Point and issued to cadet officers. The next year all cadets turned in their crossed cannons and put castles on their caps, which remained their insignia until 1869.

The worsted pompon (often written "pompom," "pompoon" and a dozen other ways by soldiers mystified by this French word) needs explaining. As long as they had worn caps, cadets had worn

some sort of plume above them. Since 1816 it has been black, but the way it was made varied. At first these plumes were constructed of short turkey feathers fastened to a stick. In the 1820's, cadet officers — or at least the cadet captains — seem to have worn a single tall ostrich feather, though this unusual plume is nowhere mentioned in regulations.

Feather plumes were expensive and hard to keep in condition. On rainy and windy days they had to be removed from the caps. Finally, in 1840, a new

This music cover of 1852 gives the public an artist's conception of what the cadet looked like, dancing a polka while on sentry duty (!).

style of plume, made of worsted, was introduced; and this has been the kind worn by most cadets ever since. Eight inches was the height of the pompon until 1853, when it shrank to three. In 1899 the cadet pompon was restored to its old size and has remained so ever since.

Cadet officers today wear tall, black, drooping cocks' feather plumes instead of pompons. This distinction was introduced in 1842 and has not been changed. The peculiar "top knot" of smaller plumes can easily be seen in several of the pictures.

A cadet officer was and is distinguished in other ways from cadets in the ranks. First of all he wears chevrons. In 1823 cadet officers and NCO's were given the exclusive right to wear tassels hanging from their leather caps, a distinction continued apparently until the cap went out in 1839. But the two really important distinctions are the sash and the sword which have always been worn by the officers of the Corps.

In the military service the sword and sash have usually gone together. Both are symbols of the commissioned officer and of the higher ranking sergeant. Of the two the sword is by far the most important, for its meaning comes down to us from the age of chivalry when the sword was the knight's principal weapon. Men were invested with rank and property by their ruler laying his sword on their shoulders. They took oaths upon their swords as we do upon the Bible today. For a long time only "gentlemen" — men born into the "gentry" or nobility — were permitted to carry swords. Since such men were the officers of those days, the sword became the badge of the officer and remained so, long after the sword was of any practical use in battle.

The common soldier sometimes carried a sword as an actual weapon. To distinguish the officer who carried a sword as a badge of rank from the soldier

Apparently this cadet expects a formation at any moment, for he is completely uniformed while studying in his barracks. In this drawing by Cadet George H. Derby in 1842, we note that the dress cap still bears the Artillery insignia.

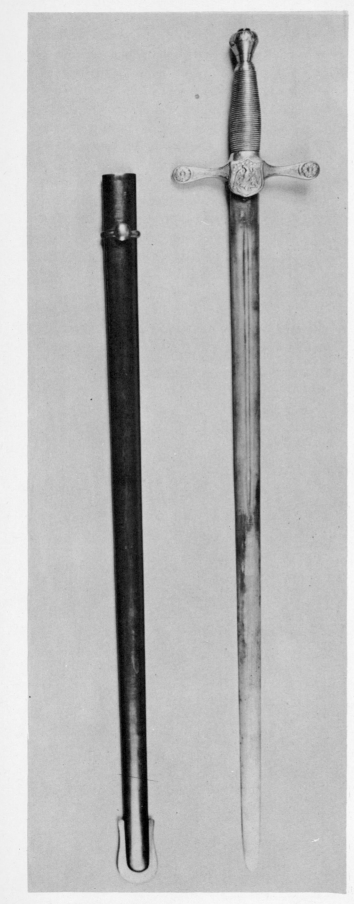

who used it to fight with, the former wore a sash. In most armies, the higher ranking sergeants were also given the right to wear swords and sashes. So the custom began — long before West Point was founded. You will hear stories that officers or sergeants wore sashes to tie up prisoners or to string between pikes to form stretchers, but these uses, if true at all, were after-thoughts.

The Board of Visitors of the Military Academy made a study of this matter in 1837, and reported to the Secretary of War that there was "a great want of swords to supply the cadets who, from time to time, act as commissioned and non-commissioned officers of their battalion. The present swords were used during the Revolution, are worn, scarcely capable of use any longer, and entirely unfitted for the purpose. A plan of a sword is understood to be in the War Department."

The Board finally recommended a new West Point sword be adopted and issued to cadet officers, and two years later, in May 1839, these new swords arrived. They were straight-bladed with a brass hilt. The guard formed a simple cross — and this fact has led to the story that they were modelled after the swords carried by the Crusaders. It is more likely that they were modelled after the style of sword carried by the Finance Corps. Two years later the Commandant ordered cadet officers always to wear the sash when the sword was worn, and specified just which sergeants were entitled to this privilege.

Twice since, the design of the cadet sword has been somewhat modified (as described later), but it still retains the simple cross design of 1839. Today the West Point cadet officer is the only man in the Army who wears a sword and sash, the sole guardian of the tradition.

The Class of 1835 introduced another symbol of West Point, the Class Ring. The Ring is not a part of the uniform, but a means of identification of a West Pointer who is not in uniform. The Military Academy was the first school in this country to adopt a ring.

Class Rings today are of gold and bear on one

This is the cadet sword carried from 1839 to 1872. Its blade is wide and straight, and its entire hilt is brass. The scabbard is of blued iron.

WEST POINT CADETS AND CADET OFFICERS, WITH BOY, 1842

The officers in the background wear the newly-adopted Engineer castles and cock's feathers on their caps. The cadet with the pompon has not yet changed the Artillery insignia on his cap, and the other cadet wears a forage cap.

One of the earliest photographs of a West Point cadet. This shows H. S. Putnam, Class of 1857, holding an ivory-headed cane. These were popular with cadets from the 1850's through the 1870's and led to some bitter remarks about the "dandies" at West Point.

Here we get our first clear view of the gray forage cap and gray overcoat as seen in a lithograph in the *U.S. Military Magazine* of January, 1841. This was a period of much experimentation in belts; the set on the right-hand cadet is unusual and was not worn after 1840.

On Post.   Full Dress.   Fatigue Dress

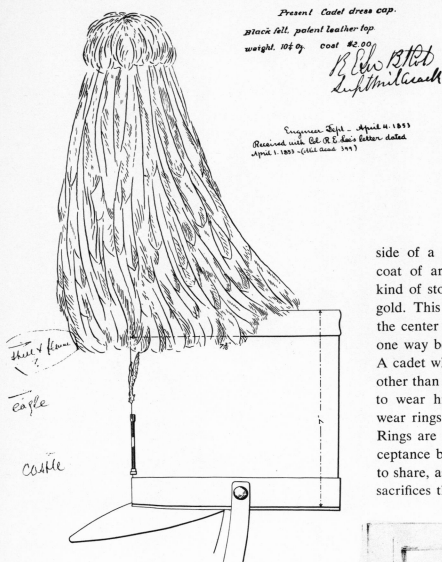

Present Cadet dress cap.

Black felt, patent leather top.

weight. 10¼ oz.   cost $2.00

R Edw Btliss
Supt Mil Acad

Engineer Dept — April 4. 1853
Received with Col R E Lee's letter dated
April 1. 1853 -(Mil Acad 399)

thill & flame 1.

Eagle

Castle

When Colonel Robert E. Lee was Superintendent of the Academy, he proposed a new dress cap for cadets in place of the "stovepipe" style. This drawing of an officer's model 7 inches high, with Lee's own handwritten notes, shows the style then in use with his suggestions for change.

side of a stone the class crest, on the other the coat of arms of the Academy. Cadets select the kind of stone they want as well as the color of the gold. This ring, its presentation and its wear, are the center of a host of traditions. The ring is worn one way before graduation and reversed thereafter. A cadet who is separated from the Academy under other than honorable circumstances forfeits the right to wear his ring and cadets are not expected to wear rings from other institutions. Miniature Class Rings are given as engagement rings, and their acceptance by a girl is taken to mean her willingness to share, as an Army wife, the ideals, traditions and sacrifices that the Class Ring symbolizes.

Every cadet recites every day in every class. This practice was begun in 1820 and still is true. Here we see a cadet with pointer in hand performing his blackboard exercises. At this period the dress coat, without accouterments, was the classroom uniform.

Although regulations strictly prohibited mustaches, Cadet Captain Gouverneur K. Warren, Class of 1850, is sporting one in this picture taken in that year. His cadet sword is slung from a white shoulder belt which has no plate.

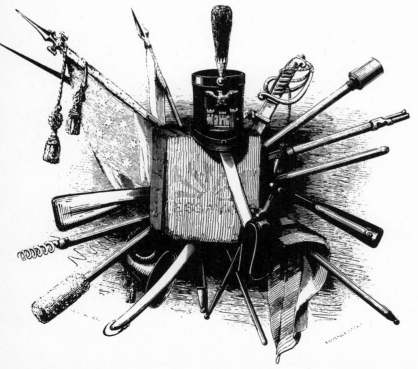

The dress hat with its worsted pompon worn from 1843 to 1854 is shown clearly in this panoply of arms used on a U.S.M.A. form in the 1840's and 50's.

Fatigue and Foul Weather Clothing

One of the characteristics of the American soldier is that he likes to do his campaigning and fighting in old, comfortable clothes. He will proudly wear a dress uniform on parade but he wants to get out of it as soon as he can. Although this may be the case with soldiers of all nations, it is especially true of United States soldiers.

Actually, therefore, full dress uniforms are worn only a small part of the time, and this is true even at West Point. Most of his day the cadet spends in some sort of field service, classroom or fatigue uniform which is far more comfortable than the full dress.

There was not as much simple clothing worn prior to the Civil War as there is now, but there was some. We read of "fatigue jackets and trousers" being issued cadets as early as 1819. These were of rough gray or sky blue wool in winter and unbleached cotton in summer. They were worn for "fatigue" duties, that is military labor distinct from the use of arms.

At that time, cadets off duty at the Military Academy could wear civilian clothing, much as an Army officer does today. But in 1821 Major Thayer issued positive orders that civilian clothing was not

When James A. McNeill Whistler was a cadet at West Point, he showed his talent with numerous drawings. This one, entitled "Asleep on the Post," drawn about 1852, shows a sentinel with the Army regulation blue cloth cap, used at West Point for a few years. Whistler never graduated.

This lithograph from a West Point song book, dated 1848, gives a fairly accurate idea of the winter uniforms worn. The gray overcoat worn by the cadet on the left was considerably shorter than the 1955 model. (Compare also with the picture on page 41.)

to be worn except on furlough off the West Point reservation, and this is still the rule. For a time an exception had to be made in headdress, and cadets either wore the older "round hats" or bought their own sporting caps to wear off duty. In 1825 a gray cloth "forage" cap was issued, and the motley array of civilian hats came to an end.

The forage cap is so called because it was originally worn in Europe by soldiers who were swarming over ("foraging") the countryside, looking for food for themselves, fodder for their horses, and perhaps other things. It was not the sort of work one did in a dress uniform, and soldiers wore their least conspicuous clothes. The name stuck to any simple cap worn on work parties and informal occasions.

For a few years (1834-1840) the forage caps were made of soft goat-skin instead of cloth. These odd-looking headdresses could be folded flat and carried in a knapsack. They were both practical and comfortable, but they were not very military, and were given up in favor of the old cloth cap.

Today every soldier is issued an overcoat, but such was not always the custom at West Point. Regiments kept a small supply of "watch coats" on hand for the sentinels on post in winter, but that was all. Overcoats were first issued to cadets at West Point in November 1828; before that they wore any kind they pleased. "Such a mixture of scotch-plaid and camlet cloaks, and cloth surtouts," one graduate recalled, "was probably never elsewhere seen on any parade."

Superintendent Thayer saw that the rigorous winters at West Point necessitated a sturdy overcoat. The one he adopted in 1828 was very much like the long overcoat worn today, except that it was single-breasted. It was a "surtout" (overall) of gray cloth, reaching down to within four inches of the ankle, with a long cape, lined with black satinette. The gilt buttons for it were flat and bore the word "CADET" on them — the first distinctive button to be worn by cadets at the Military Academy.

Vests (or "waistcoats") were an indispensable part of the uniform at this time, and continued to

1852.

This sentimental scene was drawn by Cadet Whistler in 1852, and is quite different from his other work. Note the percussion cap box on the cadet's waist belt. The officer on the left has a blue frock coat which was authorized to be worn without insignia by cadets on furlough after 1848.

(Below) A scene on Flirtation Walk drawn presumably from memory by Cadet James W. Abert in 1842.

be, as late as 1836. When the coat was buttoned all the way down, the vest was not visible, but since the coat was usually left open when off duty, the vest was a necessity. It was of gray cloth in winter and white cotton in summer.

A part of cadet clothing not known today was the stock. This uncomfortable article had been worn as far back as the Revolutionary War and even earlier, for the double purpose, as a military dictionary defined it, "of keeping the cold out and the soldier's head up." It was made of black leather for enlisted men and cadets, and of black silk for officers. It is from the leather stock that our Marines were called "Leathernecks" by the sailors aboard ship, whose collars were open. The soldier adjusted the stock around his neck (so that an edge of his shirt collar appeared over the top) and fastened it on by one or more buckles. It played a real part in

In this photo of Cadet W. H. Bell, Class of 1857, we see the riding jacket adopted in 1849. The lowered chinstrap, rakish blue cap, gauntlets and heavy saber are akin to the uniform of the hard-bitten Army cavalrymen serving in the Far West at the time.

the days when the coat collar was very large and worn open. But in 1823 when the collar was brought in tighter around the neck and hooked up, the stock no longer was visible. Nevertheless, it was a required item of wear until about 1862.

Like overcoats, gloves were a rarity among American soldiers from the Revolutionary period through the early nineteenth century. Officers wore white gloves on parade, mounted men wore gauntlets because they had to handle the reins, and mittens were served out to sentinels on cold days. But infantrymen were not issued gloves and other cold weather clothing because they rarely fought a war in winter. As soon as cold weather arrived the armies usually went into winter quarters, and re-

mained there until spring. That is why Washington's maneuver on Christmas Day of 1776 was so unusual and so successful. Crossing the Delaware River in a snowstorm was so unexpected an act that he easily caught the Hessian soldiers in Trenton off their guard.

Sometime in the early 1820's, the cadets at West Point were issued white leather gloves for dress parade, guard mounts and inspections. It must have been a striking novelty. Ever since then white gloves have been worn for full dress, although since 1835 they have been made of cotton.

It is from this era, 1820-1860, and until after the Civil War, that we get the many stories of Benny Havens. In the early 1820's, Havens opened

The collars of the cadets in all of the 1857 pictures have the V-opening introduced in 1852, and beneath this can be seen the bombasine stock. This is a photo of Cadet Captain Ira Wallace Claflin in a blue forage cap such as was worn during the 1850's.

a tavern near the post where he served, among other things, wheat cakes and a famous hot (and strong) drink called a flip. Benny's was definitely off-limits for cadets, but some managed to sneak out at night and enjoy a feast there. The oldest of all West Point songs tells the legend of Benny Havens, and its last verse (sung to the tune of "The Wearin' o' the Green") runs:

May the army be augmented,
   may promotion be less slow,
May our country in the hour of need
   be ready for the foe;
May we find a soldier's resting place
   beneath a soldier's blow,
With room enough beside our graves
   for Benny Havens, Oh!

In the 1850's and '60's

When we reach the 1850's we come to the era of the photograph, and from the pictures taken at West Point we gain a more intimate knowledge of how the cadets dressed and looked. Beginning in 1857, each graduating class stood before the camera, individually and in groups, and all of these photographs have been preserved.

The photos of the Class of 1857 show the changes that came about in uniforms and accouterments just prior to the Civil War. Cadet Lieutenant R. H. Anderson has beside him on the table, the new model dress cap adopted in 1853. Its narrow, sloping top is very much in the fashion of the day, corresponding in form to the style adopted by the Army at large in 1851. Colonel Robert E. Lee, Superintendent from 1852 to 1855, had successfully urged the adoption of this cap in place of the "stovepipe" style worn since 1839. The eagle and Engineer castle, it will be noted, continued unchanged.

All of the photographs show the new "V" cut of the collar, a great advance in comfort, introduced in June 1852. This illustrates the general loosening of the uniform from the stiff, tight styles of the

On the table next to Cadet Lieutenant R. H. Anderson, Class of 1857, is the cap introduced by Superintendent Robert E. Lee four years earlier. This carries a black cock's feather plume. Anderson was photographed in summer Full Dress without arms.

In this picture of Cadet Samuel W. Ferguson, Class of 1857, we see two unusual things: he is wearing an oil cover on his forage cap, allowed only on rainy days; also, his coat is open. The open coat was much in fashion (although not permitted under arms) as it gave the cadet a chance to insert his right hand in Napoleonic fashion! Ferguson became a general in the Confederacy.

1830's and 1840's, which had been the most notoriously uncomfortable decades in all the history of military dress. As early as 1843 the Superintendent had begun a fight against tight clothing, ordering that coats and pantaloons worn by cadets be cut full enough "to give great freedom and ease to the wearer." He particularly wanted loose clothes worn in "the athletic exercises of football, Riding, Artillery drill, Light Infantry drill, sword exercises, etc.," and to "inculcate the opinion among the Cadets that tight clothing is not military."

The cadets did not need much inculcation in that direction. Soon coat collars were being left unhooked to expose flowing black cravats — a fashion especially popular at "cotillions," as the hops of those days were called. Some cadets sported shirts with romantic "Byron collars" while off duty.

And the fashion of leaving open two or three center buttons of the coat took an especially strong hold. Cadet Ferguson was only one of many who left coats open; this was to allow the cadet, at appropriate times, to stick his right hand through the opening in imitation of Napoleon!

Against such transgressions the orders stormed and the Tactical Officers passed out demerits. Tactical Officers, assigned to the Department of Tactics, are responsible for the training of cadets in military skills, discipline, drill, etc. But freedom was in the air in the late 1840's. Once again Europe had been swept with revolutions which had radically altered the style of military dress. The principal Army casualty now was the old tailcoat, although the Corps of Cadets did not succumb to this change. By then the gray tailcoat with its bullet buttons had become such a tradition that it was allowed to remain. After about 1851, however, West Point was the only place in the Regular Army in which it could be found.

The men's hair as seen in the 1857 photographs, is in the full style popular during the decade just before the Civil War. In some cases, cadets wore their hair as long as a girl would wear hers today. It was perfectly permissible — for hair on a soldier's face and head was regulated as carefully as the buttons on his coat, especially at West Point. In the Army at large, the War Department usually fought a (losing) battle against fashions in hair, but at the Military Academy control was far more strict. The orderly books of the nineteenth century are filled with restrictions against hair on the lip, or under the chin, or somewhere else, and the punishment lists show numerous charges like "unshaven

Cadets and femmes at a "hop" in about 1859. The dance is probably a waltz. Note the chaperone, the two cadets in the stag line, the Officer of the Day (with sash over right shoulder), the hop managers in sashes, and one couple dancing head-to-cheek. From *Harper's Weekly*.

on parade," "not cutting off his whiskers," and "too long hair."

Much to the distaste of the Corps, the men's hair was first ordered to be cut short in February 1826. Thereafter, every cadet had to report to the barber once a month at a specified time. Four years later the Superintendent ordered that "the barber will in future regulate the manner of cutting Cadet's hair according to special directions given him by the Commandant of the Corps, to which uniformity the taste or fancy of individuals must necessarily acquiesce." Thus hair styles were regulated from above and so it remains today. But regulation styles are styles nonetheless, and at times, Army officers have been known to go to extremes in this direction. Only thus can we account for the occasional mustaches or long locks seen on some cadets.

One of the earliest organized sports was horseback riding. Training in riding and the care of horses began in 1839. Cavalry was still fairly new in the Army for it had been brought back only six years before. For 18 years a parsimonious Con-

A cadet "firing at the head," or mounted exercise with the pistol, in the Riding Hall about 1855. This engraving is from *Scribner's Monthly,* July 1872.

gress had avoided paying the heavy cost of mounted troops. But as the fringe of white settlements reached the Plain country west of the Mississippi, we met mounted Indians and found our slow moving infantry unable to catch them. Congress then established what is now our oldest cavalry regiment, the First Dragoons. When the time came for a cadet to go to the riding ring, he put on his oldest uniform, making certain his trousers were held down by a strap under the instep. Over his ankles he strapped a pair of heavy Dragoon spurs, and on his head he put the smallest cap he could find.

He also had to carry "Old Wrist Breaker," as the immense Dragoon saber of that time was called. This was buckled to a special black leather waist belt, introduced in 1839 for wear by cadets taking equitation. Then, ten years later simple gray jackets with eight buttons, together with a pair of reinforced trousers were given cadets. Buckskin gauntlets followed in 1850, so that the cadet on horseback put on a pretty faithful imitation of those rakish Dragoons who had just carved out such a reputation for themselves on the battlefields of Mexico. Thus is Cadet W. H. Bell garbed in the photograph on page 47.

In the 1857 photos, we see how the Corps, some 278 strong in those days, was dressed in the years just before the Civil War. Eighty-six of this number had come from the South when, in late 1860 and early 1861, the Southern states drew away from the Union to form the Confederacy. Of these cadets, 65 resigned rather than take up arms against their native states, 21 remained with the Union side. It was a sad, confusing period, which saw the breaking of deep friendships. Some men at the time considered the cadets from the South

Looking south from the Military Academy in the Civil War period. West Point covers the approach along the Hudson from three directions.

ADJUTANT, U.S. CORPS OF CADETS, WITH INSTRUCTOR, 1862

Like cadet officers today, the cadet officer in Civil War times wore the tall, black, drooping cock's feather plumes, instead of the pompon. This distinction, introduced in 1842, has not been changed since. The officer in the background belongs to the Corps of Engineers.

The fatigue uniform of gray shell jackets and forage caps is shown by the two cadets in the rear in this wood engraving from *Gleason's Pictorial*, 1852.

This artillery drill is apparently being carried out in dress uniform in 1852. The artist is on questionable ground in including belts over the right shoulder in this wood engraving from *Gleason's Pictorial*.

A panorama of cadet life at West Point in July, 1868. Reading clockwise, from left top, are a cavalry charge on the Plain, Kosciuszko's Monument, salute to school ships from Battery Knox, fencing, telegraphing, cadet limits, practical military engineering, examination before Board of Visitors, mortar practice, section room, "Stand attention, sir!", reporting to the Adjutant; and in the center, presentation of diplomas by General Ulysses S. Grant.

(Above) The siege battery with its guns aimed north, in 1869. Note the ammunition piled neatly alongside each cannon.

(Below) In this drawing by Cadet Whistler we see the dress cap adopted in 1853. This is one of a set of four drawings Whistler made of a cadet on sentry duty, and this is entitled "Second Half Hour."

as unfaithful to their trust, indeed, as traitors. But this was only the opinion of men who did not have to make that terrible decision.

When the four-year struggle ended, all of the armies in the field on both sides were commanded by graduates of the Military Academy. There was hardly an important battle fought that did not have one side, and usually both, commanded by a West Pointer. Familiar names like Ulysses S. Grant, Robert E. Lee, "Stonewall" Jackson, George B. McClellan, William T. Sherman, and James Longstreet all belonged to graduates of the Military Academy. In all, 445 graduates reached general's rank in one army or another. Such was West Point's record.

The Academy at Mid-Period

In the thirty years or so from the end of the Civil War to the outbreak of the War with Spain in 1898, there were few striking changes in the cadet uniform and, for that matter, few in the Military Academy itself. However, there was one very important innovation at the very start. In 1866, when Colonel Thomas G. Pitcher of the Infantry became Superintendent of the Academy, it was the first time a man who was not an Engineer had been appointed. A new law had made this assignment possible, and the 62-year-long connection of West Point with the Corps of Engineers was broken.

To signalize the change, in 1869 the Engineer castle was removed from the dress cap. In its place a brass sunburst with a shield in its center was used, and on this shield were embossed the insignia of the four combat arms: Engineers, Artillery, Cavalry and Infantry. The Military Academy thus proclaimed itself the school for all the Army.

A cadet has always been permitted to select the arm or branch of the service to which he will be assigned after graduation, but his ability to choose

Reveille comes at 5:50 A.M. at West Point and 10 minutes later comes Assembly. This scene drawn by Julian Scott about 1870 shows the West Point Army Detachment wearing dark blue frock coats and forage caps, with sky-blue trousers.

depends on his general standing in his class. There are just so many openings in each branch; and the Number One cadet has the first choice, Number Two next, and so on down to the "Anchor Man" who has to take what is left. Before the Civil War top rankers — men like Robert E. Lee — selected the Corps of Engineers as being the elite of the branches of the service, but such a choice would not necessarily be made today.

The "sunburst" dress cap did not last long. The four arms of the service represented on it failed to include such branches as the Ordnance Department or the Signal Corps, in which West Pointers were serving. So a simple device bearing the letters "USMA," an eagle, and crossed sword and pen, was adopted in 1878. This was placed on a small dress cap — the smallest ever worn at West Point, but very fashionable at the time — and it continued in use until 1899.

Some of the photographs taken in these years

(Below) The cadets in 1869 camped in summertime on the Plain. This guard detail is in summer Full Dress with the new model dress caps. Their rifles lie crossed over the guard rack.

(Above) We see a new dress cap here, the 1869 pattern, on Cadet Lieutenant Fayette Roe, Class of 1871. His brass belt-plate is rounded to fit over a button.

(Above) These cadets are waiting to carry the colors at summer camp in 1883. (Below) Cadet uniforms of about 1883. On the extreme right is the First Captain in summer Full Dress. The men in the center wear small dark blue forage caps of the "chasseur" model adopted in 1861. Note also the turnover shirt collar still in use at the time.

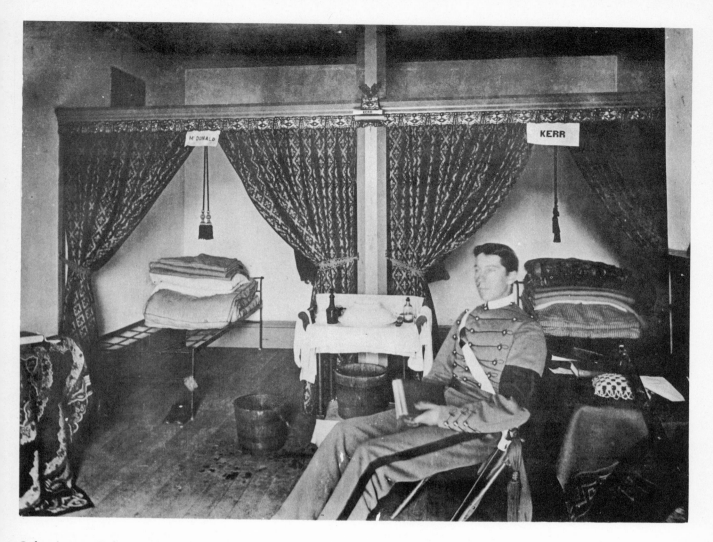

Cadets in 1870 had washstands in their rooms but they had to carry water from a pump, as evidenced by the buckets shown here. This room had draperies, tassels, and pincushions in keeping with the decor of the Victorian era. The mattresses and blankets are folded in true military style.

show cadets with double the regulation amount of braid and buttons on their dress coats. These men held appointments as Acting Assistant Professors. To supplement the often meager teaching staff at the Academy it had long been the practice to appoint high standing cadets to teach the others. They drew higher pay and in 1823 were authorized to wear 14 instead of 8 rows of buttons on their coats, as a mark of distinction. The extra braid and buttons were merely sewn on between the others. It is interesting to note that this practice, after long disuse, had to be revived during the Second World War. On that occasion the cadet instructors were allowed to wear brass Academy coats of arms on

their collars, the buttons on the full dress collar being removed for the purpose.

Unlike most schools and colleges, cadets at West Point are not called Seniors, Juniors, Sophomores and Freshmen, but fourth year men are known as "First Classmen"; those in the third year, "Second Classmen" or "Cows"; sophomores are "Yearlings," and freshmen, "Plebes." In 1899, in order to tell one class from another, narrow stripes of braid were sewn on the sleeves of the dress and full dress coat, and in 1910, these were sewn on the overcoat as well.

Three stripes indicated a First Classman; two a Second Classman, and one, a Yearling. The sleeves of a Plebe were left bare. At a much later date the system of identification was extended to include the shirt, by means of colored shields on the collar.

The long gray overcoat, which had been made double-breasted in 1851, has become a traditional part of the cadets' uniform. It has been copied by

military schools throughout the country. In some schools its cape is lined with red, or blue, or some other color, like the officers' capes of the Old Army, but at West Point it is plain. This cape is normally worn thrown back over the shoulders. Plebes, however, must wear it down in front except when under arms, marching to football games, and at a few other prescribed times.

You may hear the story that to wear red-lined capes a military corps must first have shed blood in action, but this is only one of the many fables entwined with cadet gray. The corps of cadets at the Virginia Military Institute does wear red linings and it has shed blood in battle, but the reason for the simplicity of West Point capes lies in the desire not to display a color which would be associated with a particular branch of the Army, such as blue for Infantry, scarlet for Artillery, or yellow for Cavalry (now Armor).

Closely allied to the cadet uniform are the Colors carried by the Corps. The word "colors"

Cadets in a street parade in New York about 1889, turning the corner into East 15th Street, just off Union Square. The sergeants acting as right guides carry their rifles at the "shoulder," while the others use "right shoulder shift."

distinguishes the special silken flags borne by Army regiments and battalions on parade from other kinds of flags, and derives from the days when regiments were given distinctively colored flags to represent their colonel or some other person. In the American regular service, Army organizations usually have carried two colors, one, the National — standing for the United States; and the other, the Organizational (Corps, Battalion, etc.), which stands for the unit itself. These are a military unit's most precious symbols; if only one color is carried, it must combine the symbolism of both the National and Organizational. The Corps has carried colors since the City of Boston gave it two beautifully painted flags in 1821. From then on, for about twenty years, the Corps carried two Colors — on one flag was painted the national coat of arms

WHITE FATIGUES AND SUMMER AND FULL DRESS AT WEST POINT, 1885

For ordinary work at Summer Camp, cadets wore white linen fatigue trousers and jackets during the day. With these went a cork sun helmet, covered with white cloth. For dress purposes the Corps received brass spikes and chains to put on the helmets, as seen in the picture. The cadet on the right wears the "50-50" full dress.

The National Color carried 1890-93, which was typical of the single color carried by the Corps after 1870.

(Above) This dark blue silk flag was the Corps Color, 1894-1897, and was carried with the Stars and Stripes until replaced by the gray type in 1902.

which stood for the Country and the other bore a device symbolic of the Military Academy. Apparently from 1841 to 1894 only one Color was carried. At first it was dark blue with the national coat of arms, and later it became the Stars and Stripes, on whose center red stripe was painted in gold letters, the words "U. S. Corps of Cadets." The practice of two colors was resumed in 1894.

Colors are carried by specially selected Color Sergeants. These men are guarded by two sergeants and followed by four more, who stand ready to take over a flag should its bearer fall. This practice stems from the days when regiments carried their colors openly in battle. Color bearers were favorite targets for the enemy, and sometimes ten or more men were shot from under a flag in a single fight.

At West Point, the Colors are carried on parade upright and partially furled, whereas the rest of the Army carry them flying. Only when passing in review are the Corps Colors allowed to fly free.

(Right) On the West Point reservation today, the military police of the 1802d Special Regiment raise the post garrison flag as shown in this striking picture.

Changing Weapons

The belts, boxes and other accouterments soldiers wear have, from the beginning, been brought about or modified by the weapons they have had to handle. To a great degree the same can be said about their clothing. When, in the late 1600's, hand grenades came into use, the men who threw them found they knocked off their wide cocked hats. They were given narrow caps as a result, from which developed the tall grenadier bearskins now worn by the Guardsmen who stand in the sentry boxes at Buckingham Palace. When the revolver came into common usage on our frontier, men found it wise to carry one in their belts. Thus developed, in the 1850's, the modern pistol holster and the technique of gun play.

The cadet's accouterments were in like manner affected by his weapons. A few of these, the first French muskets and the cadet sword, have been mentioned already. These were only the beginning of a long line of such arms.

The first muskets carried were flintlock muzzle-loaders, almost as tall as the cadets themselves. They fired a lead ball of .69 inch caliber, could be loaded and fired at the rate of two or three "rounds" a minute by a trained soldier, and were effective up to about 100 yards. The ball and a charge of black powder were wrapped together in paper to form a cartridge, which had to be bitten off before loading. A simple bayonet with a triangular blade could be fitted onto the muzzle.

Cartridges were carried in a black leather box which usually hung on the rear of the soldier's right hip, while the bayonet rested on the other hip. Both were suspended from belts passing over the men's shoulders which, crossing on the chest and back, were called "cross" or "shoulder belts." These belts were at first made of white buff leather. White cross belts were a commonplace in all armies; they were white because, like the brass buttons, they were showy.

By 1840 webbing replaced leather for the white belts; it was cheaper and easier to keep in order. Cadets were issued a white waist belt and a "throg" or "frog," into which the bayonet scabbard was fitted, the frog sliding on the belt. This eliminated the need for a belt over the right shoulder, and cross belts disappeared from the cadet uniform until revived in 1899.

The flintlock system was replaced at West Point by the more efficient percussion lock musket in 1845, with a caliber of .57. This new system demanded a place to carry the percussion caps. One answer was to let a small pocket into the jacket; another was to issue little boxes of black leather lined with sheepskin. As was mentioned before, the percussion boxes, by Corps order, were worn on the waist belt exactly "one inch from the right edge of the waist plate."

In the earlier days, there was always a problem of furnishing shorter and lighter muskets for the "g-nomies" (gee-nomies), the smaller cadets. A musket reaching to the chin of an average-sized man became next to impossible for the shorter boys to handle without knocking off their tall caps. Even in modern times, with the magazine rifle, a cadet must learn a special manual to avoid such accidents.

The first shorter muskets sent to West Point were odd models, clearly different from the regulation, like the ones received in 1813, which had been designed for the Indians. It is not difficult to see why these substitutes were unpopular. Eventually, in 1830, at the special request of the Superintendent, a distinctive Cadet Model flintlock musket of smaller caliber (.54) was manufactured in two

The weapons carried by the Corps in 1874 show clearly in this photo of a group of cadets in summer camp on the Plain. Stacked at the left are four single-shot, breech-loading rifles (Cadet Model 1868), and over the stack hangs a leather cart-ridge box of the period. The two standing cadets carry light cavalry sabers (Model 1860), and the officer has a cadet sword (Model 1872). The cadets are wearing the "chasseur" model forage caps, and the officer the 1869 model cap with plume.

sizes and shipped to the Academy. Thereafter, until the first magazine rifle was authorized in 1892, special cadet models of the different firearms were procured for West Point.

Two minor changes in the cadet musket (Models 1851 and 1858) followed and then the breech-loading rifle, using a metallic cartridge, arrived in 1867. It was a .50 caliber weapon taking a center fire, black powder cartridge. Although single shot, it was a real improvement over the old muzzle-loader. A soldier now could take cover on the ground while he loaded and fired, and he could fire from two to three times faster and more accurately. Such an increase in firepower foreshadowed the

end of the old close-order formations, in which men stood up, elbow-to-elbow, and traded volleys with the enemy. Indeed, it pointed to a complete change in Infantry tactics; and from this period forward, drill on the parade ground no longer prepared soldiers for maneuvers in the field.

Not long after metallic cartridges came into use, men started to look for better ways to carry them than in the old leather cartridge boxes. Two meth-ods resulted. One was the looped cartridge belt, about which more will be said. The other was a leather box invented by Captain Samuel McKeever, 2d Infantry, which was adopted by the Army in the 1880's. This box held 20 cartridges.

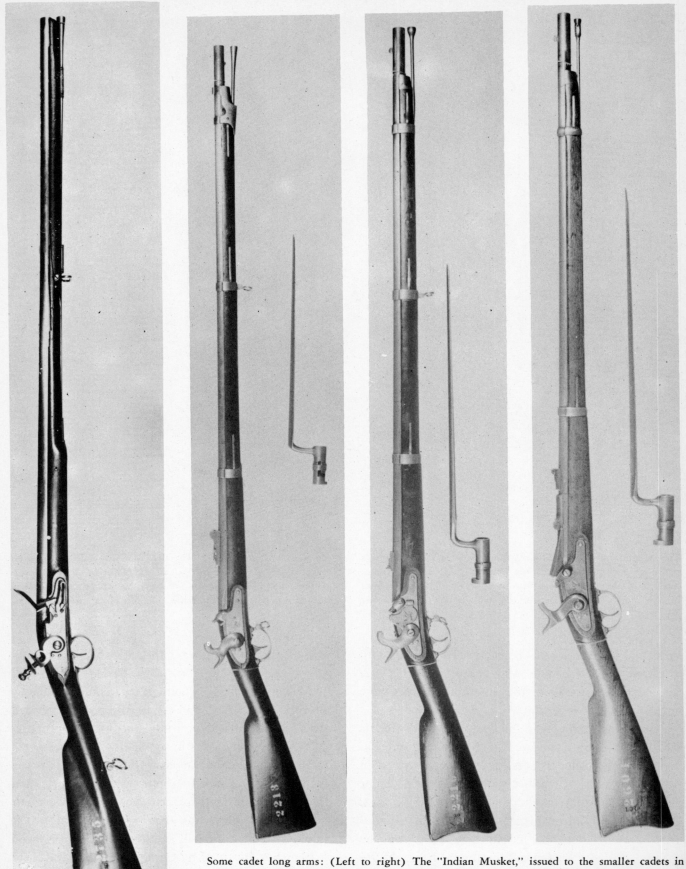

Some cadet long arms: (Left to right) The "Indian Musket," issued to the smaller cadets in 1813; Cadet Musket Model 1851, a smoothbore, single-shot, percussion muzzle-loader; Cadet Musket Model 1858, a rifled, single-shot, percussion muzzle-loader; Cadet Rifle Model 1868, a rifled, single-shot, metallic cartridge, breech-loader.

(Above) "Rally to the colors" is the name given to this formation. When R. F. Zogbaum drew this in 1886 the formation was already outmoded, and a few years later the magazine rifle's introduction took it completely out of the drill manual.

(Below) Field artillery drill on the Plain in the summer of 1879. The cannoneers are probably Plebes, wearing gray shell jackets. By each gun stands an upperclassman in full dress coat. The guns are 12-pounder Napoleons.

(Above) Cavalry drill and tactics were taught at West Point for 108 years — from 1839 to 1947. In this photo we see the cadet troop drawn up for inspection on the Plain in about 1903.

(Below) Volley firing with the first magazine rifle to reach West Point, the Krag-Jorgensen, about 1899. The cadets wear web looped cartridge belts and short Krag knife bayonets.

The McKeever was received at West Point and for a few years was used to hold cartridges. But after the loop belt arrived, the box became a strictly full dress item, fastened to a white shoulder belt, dyed black and kept highly polished. Since cartridges are no longer carried on dress parade, "drags" (girls invited to the Point for dances) often want to know what is kept in "that cute little box." The answer today is simple: "Nothing — it isn't a box." In years past cadets (against regulations) stored things like an emergency button or a piece of chocolate in the McKeever, but then someone got the idea of fitting in a block of wood to give it shape. In time the supply of McKeevers (long obsolete in the Army) ran out and today the box is nothing more than a block of wood covered with leather.

After using about five models of the single-shot weapon (most being caliber .45) the Corps of Cadets received the magazine rifle in 1895. This completed the change in tactics brought on by the

This is not a prison camp, but simply the butts on the rifle range at West Point, about 1900. The cadets are awaiting their turn to practice the new kind of marksmanship made possible by the Krag-Jorgensen magazine rifle. The range was 200 yards and more.

breech-loader, and all over the world armies abandoned close order drill for fighting. The first magazine rifle to reach West Point was the Krag-Jorgensen, which loaded through a gate on the right side of the receiver. Its caliber was .30, much smaller than ever before tried, and it fired a smokeless powder cartridge. The bayonet was the knife type, the first to be carried at West Point.

Sometime in 1905 the Corps turned in its Krags and drew the new Model 1903, commonly called the "Springfield" or "03." The first of these excellent weapons carried an unfortunate ramrod bayonet, but this was changed to a knife type the same year. The "03" was carried until replaced by the present semi-automatic M-1 in 1940.

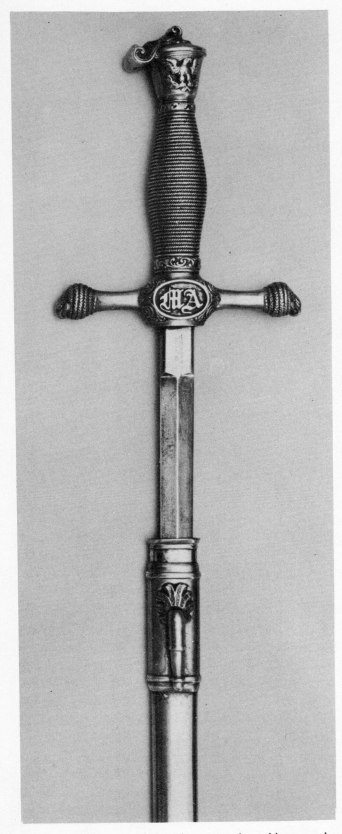

A change in weapons came in 1872 when this somewhat different model of cadet sword was adopted. It retained the simple lines of the 1839 sword, but had a narrower blade and a loop for holding a sword knot.

The third and current model of cadet sword was introduced about 1923. Unlike the 1872 model, the hilt of this sword is not *entirely* of brass—the grip is of white metal. Note that the letters "MA" have been replaced by the Academy Coat of Arms.

Classrooms and Summer Camps

To become a successful officer a cadet must be familiar with tactics and techniques of the combat arms, and he must be strong in body and hardy in spirit. So he spends many hours during the summer at Camp Buckner, in the hills back of West Point, firing all the weapons, bivouacking in the open, and just plain marching like any other dogface (infantryman). Every year sees two classes in summer camp: the new First and Third. While they are there, the Plebes who have just arrived at the Academy are given over to the careful supervision of "New Cadet Details" of First Classmen, and the new Second Class goes on a field trip to other installations.

Before the Corps spent its summers at Camp Buckner, it used to camp on the Plain, a few hundred yards from the barracks. It was a pretty soft kind of camp, but it was combined with field exercises and bivouacs around the countryside. For ordinary work in summer the cadets were given

In this more or less "candid" picture taken in the summer of 1883, we see the various styles of cadet uniform including the long overcoat (cadet in doorway) and the white parade uniform (cadet on extreme left).

(Above) Cadets and their "drags" on a seacoast cannon on Trophy Point, about 1880.

(Below) In this summer camp group of 1875, we see gray riding uniforms, white fatigues, and full dress grays over white.

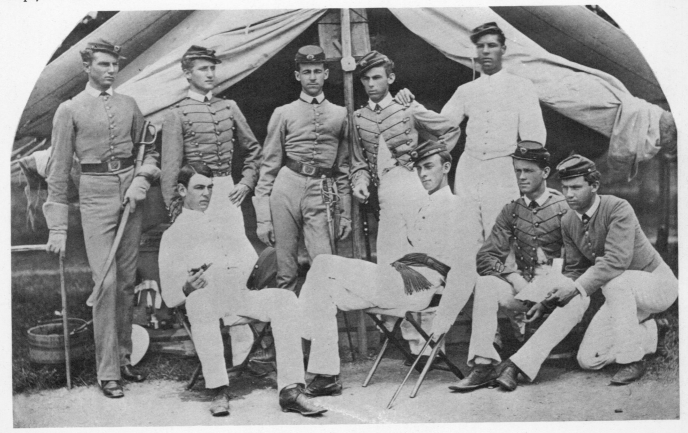

These cadets may look relaxed but they really are not. If we look closely, we see that they are carefully keeping their white trousers off the dirt by sitting on folded campstools while their femmes (chaperoned, of course) try to look modest. In the right rear stands the Cadet Officer of the Day, as shown by the sash in part over his right shoulder. Summer camp, 1875.

white linen fatigue trousers and jackets which they wore during the day. With these went a cork sun helmet, covered with white cloth. No insignia was worn on this white uniform, but in 1881 the Corps received brass spikes and chains to put on the helmets for dress purposes.

The adoption of the spiked helmet — not only at West Point but throughout the Army at large — shows how powerful military styles can be. Up to the 1870's most fashions in uniforms had come from France, for the French army was considered the paragon. Then, to the astonishment of almost everyone, the German army delivered it a crushing defeat in 1870-1871, in the Franco-Prussian War. A new military star had risen. All eyes turned towards Germany, where the spiked helmet had been the military hat for over 25 years. Within a short time, spiked helmets were in fashion and had been adopted by at least half the armies of the world. Great Britain (including Canada) introduced them in 1878, the United States in 1881, and within ten years they were being worn by troops in lands as far apart as Australia and Portugal, Brazil and Norway.

In 1889, a gray blouse, trimmed down the front, around the bottom and up the back, with black mohair braid, one inch wide, was adopted to replace the gray shell and riding jackets. This same coat or blouse (called Dress Gray) is worn today as a semi-dress uniform with either white or gray trousers. For many years after 1889, it was the coat the cadet knew best, for he wore it to class and for most of the day.

(Above) Drill in the Siege Battery, 1885. The cadets wear gray riding jackets and blue forage caps.

(Below) Guard mount at summer camp, 1888. This type full dress cap was adopted ten years earlier.

In 1889 also came the passing of the turn-down shirt collar, and its replacement by a starched white collar which could be attached inside the collar of the coat to show ⅜ inch (no more, no less) over the top. Rubberized raincoats (called "mackintoshes") came in 1894 to supplement the gray overcoats.

The forage cap was still the flat dark blue "chasseur" model we usually associate with the Civil War. It had been adopted in 1861, and until 1867 was worn without a device. In that year, after a little experimentation, an embroidered insignia showing "USMA" over an eagle in flight was adopted for it.

By now the cadet had three distinct types of uniform: full dress, dress, and all white fatigues. As always, he bought these out of an allowance granted him by the Government. Although he owned only a single full dress, the chances were that he kept several sets of the other uniforms in his room, and cases of cadets owning twenty or more pair of white trousers are not uncommon.

White fatigues and helmets were regulation uniform for cadets in field artillery drill in 1894. Note the ballet-dancer stance of the cadets as they load the cannon. The muzzle loader was still in use at this period.

Old or new, every piece had to be in perfect shape and at any time could be ruled out by a Tactical Officer. In general, only washable items could be passed on to other cadets. Thus, a First Classman, about to graduate, had to practice great economy and care lest he should end his career at West Point with a large surplus of uniforms and a depleted allowance account.

The arrival, in 1895, of the magazine rifle was the signal for a fourth uniform. With this weapon the battle range of Infantry fire jumped to over 600 yards, and to rates like 30 shots a minute. Officers were looking with greater interest at Gatling guns and especially at a fully automatic weapon invented ten years before by Hiram Maxim. Until this time the range of muskets had been so short that it made no difference what color uniform a soldier wore. But now the need for specially designed and protectively colored "field service" uniforms was beginning to be understood, and all over the world armies began to experiment with loose-fitting, drab-colored clothing, and with accouterments that would permit the solder to carry increased loads of ammunition.

The Spanish-American War of 1898 forced the War Department to act. In 1899, cadets at West

(Above, left) Rear view of the first field service uniform at West Point, adopted in 1898. (Right) A change in field service dress was made by about 1904. A Montana peak replaced the crease in the campaign hat. The belt is a woven pattern adopted by the Army in 1903 to permit clips of cartridges to be carried.

Point were issued their first field service uniform. It comprised a gray campaign hat creased down the center, gray woolen shirt, gray trousers, leggings and the full Army field equipment. Among the items were a canvas looped cartridge belt, blanket

(Right) When studying surveying, these cadets of 1907 wear
gray fatigue coats (blouses)
with black mohair braid, which
in 1889 had replaced the riding
jacket. The gray cap was introduced in 1903. The single small
stripe on their cuffs indicates
they are Yearlings.

(Below) Saturday inspection in
summer camp, 1895. Here the
white spiked helmet is being
worn with the full dress coat.

(Right) In the Electricity Lab in 1905. Before the days of the tailored shirt, Dress Gray was the uniform for class. The nearest cadet is a First Classman and a lieutenant.

(Right, below) In the art classroom in 1905. In this one class, cadets were required to remove their coats, a practice that continued for many years. Curiously, the collars and cuffs were not attached to the shirts, but to the coats!

roll, entrenching tool and canteen — apparently the first true campaign gear ever to be worn by the Corps. At about this same time the Army at large adopted its first khaki clothing.

From this point on, the West Point field service uniform and its accouterments changed constantly as new items were developed, tested and adopted by the Army. The creased campaign hat was given up for one with the Montana peak, then readopted, then given up once more. Canvas leggings were followed by puttees of black leather. The blanket roll and haversack were replaced by the Model 1910 web equipment with its "long pack." And the straight gray trousers with black stripes, used for so many purposes at West Point, eventually gave way for field service to gray breeches with a distinct peg. But throughout the forty-three years from the War with Spain to the Second World War, the basic field service uniform at West Point, except for one brief gap in 1918-19, remained gray.

The Uniform Looks Backward

As the Military Academy approached the turn of the century and West Point looked forward to its centennial in 1902, its officers and graduates were stirred by a realization of West Point's position in history. In looking back over the first century of achievement, and peering forward into the future, these men were merely thinking what thousands of other thoughtful Americans were thinking about the country at large. For the closing years of the Nineteenth Century were to be years of vast importance in American history, although no one realized what momentous events were to come.

In 1898 the United States abruptly became a first-class world power, with military obligations extending across 8000 miles of ocean. War was becoming "modern," and armies were being counted in figures unheard of a generation earlier. That the Military Academy would have to expand and modernize was clear to all who paused to consider. At the same time, West Point's record over the past century proved that in matters of the mind and spirit it had a product to offer that would prove every bit as valuable in the future as it had been in the past. How to embrace the new technology without losing the old spirit was, in short, the problem.

One answer was to create symbols of the West Point spirit which would keep this spirit alive for future classes of cadets. Several steps were taken. In 1896 a committee was appointed to consider and report on a distinctive device and motto for the Academy; early in 1898 it made its recommendations: it proposed the coat of arms illustrated here as best signifying "the national character of the Academy, its military function, its educational function . . . and its characteristic spirit. . . ." The

In Heraldry, all figures should face in the direction the flag is moving. When the West Point Coat of Arms was first designed, the eagle and helmet faced in the wrong direction, and many flags had to be designed over. This is the Corps Color of the present day, with the correct facing; this particular flag was carried in the Inaugural Parade of 1953 when a famous West Point graduate was sworn in as President.

The Full Dress adopted in 1899 (seen above) was unabashedly traditional. This cadet wears both cross and waist belts, and his hat is in the style popular 50 years before, but with the new "Fried Egg" brass plate in front. His rifle is the Krag-Jorgensen.

helmet of Pallas Athene, Grecian goddess of wisdom and the arts of war, was a device already in use at West Point. The sword, the American eagle and shield, and the motto "Duty, Honor, Country," completed the arms, which were approved by the Secretary of War the same year and so became official.

It is ironical to note that, despite the great pains taken to select the best symbols and to arrange

them correctly, the new design carried an unfortunate meaning in terms of Heraldry. Both the eagle and helmet faced to the left (that is, to "sinister") and thus "backwards." It was not realized at the time, but on a coat of arms this stands for cowardice and dishonor. The old knights, who painted coats of arms on their shields, always depicted their animals and other devices facing to the right. Twenty-five years later, therefore, after much discussion, thousands of these coats of arms were changed at some cost to show the devices facing properly.

The full dress uniform in use at that time was now long out of date, and there was no way to modernize it without destroying its traditional lines. Therefore the authorities made a sound decision — they changed the Full Dress back to what it had been during its height of fashion. The new field service uniform was modern, so the Full Dress could be unabashedly traditional!

This decision led to the adoption of a full dress cap which, while not an exact copy of an older form, had at least the general feel of the early Nineteenth Century. In the process, people began to call it a "hat" rather than a "cap," while the cadets dubbed it a "tarbucket," by which it is best known. At the same time, cross belts were brought back. The McKeever cartridge box was hung now on *both* belts and the new Krag-Jorgensen bayonet, in a metal scabbard, was suspended from a waist belt. Altogether it was an artificial arrangement, unheard of in earlier days, but the three belts gave a big splash of white and their two plain brass buckles sparkled brightly in the sunlight.

The pompon was enlarged at this time to 8 inches and the new coat of arms of the Military Academy was made up into a brass plate, called by cadets the "Fried Egg," for the front of the shako. Cadet

The Colors in 1900. By this time, two flags were being carried: the National Color (with the legend "U.S. Corps of Cadets" still on the center stripe, as we see here), and the blue Corps Color, much like those carried by infantry regiments. The cadets on the right are not from the regular color party.

officers wore a single shoulder belt for the sword, a crimson sash and the same black cock's feather plume as before. With a few minor changes, this is the full dress uniform worn today.

Somewhere about the turn of the century we first hear of "Plebeskins." At West Point there is a principle, long adhered to, that every uniform a cadet wears will be fitted to him personally by master tailors. Since it was impossible to measure new cadets before their arrival in July, a supply of ready-made dress gray uniforms in several sizes was manufactured ahead of time. These were called Plebeskins and were of a lighter weight material than the regular uniform, with the coats left unlined.

Dress uniforms are still hand-tailored; and, so far as practical, all clothing is fitted individually. The Plebeskin of the present day is a pair of low-cut gray trousers with belt loops; this is worn until a heavier pair is tailored for the Plebe in the fall. Thereafter he can use his Plebeskins for gym and other less formal occasions.

The Twentieth Century, it is sorrowful to relate, brought back the "choker" collar on the gray uniforms, last seen in 1852. The change was gradual and probably unintentional, but there is still some cause for complaint. As one graduate wrote: "The collar shrinks with every cleaning, makes the cadet's

Exercise with a siege gun, about 1903, was not considered field service, but classroom work, and so the cadets wore classroom dress of gray fatigue blouse with black mohair braid, plus canvas leggings. The shirt and campaign hat were reserved for actual field service.

eyes bug out, induces boils, and makes thinking impossible." This may sound extreme, but many a cadet will bear him out.

By 1899, West Point was regularly playing other colleges in football and other sports. The need was felt for distinctive colors to represent the Military Academy teams. In that year the now famous black, gold and gray were selected — colors that had so prominently marked the uniforms of cadets since 1815. There seems to be no other reason for the choice of these colors, although you may hear the story that they represent the three ingredients of gun powder (charcoal, sulphur and saltpeter).

The adoption of a coat of arms and official colors led to a significant change in the Corps Color. From a dark blue flag with the national coat of arms it became one with a gray field on which the Academy coat of arms was embroidered in full color. Underneath was a red ribbon bearing the words "U. S. Corps of Cadets" in gold letters. The fringe was black, gray and gold. This same design is used today. (See page 77.)

With these changes the Corps of Cadets entered its second century.

WEST POINT CADETS IN FIELD SERVICE UNIFORM WITH CAVALRY DETACHMENT, 1925

The field service uniform, first issued in 1898, by this time had been changed so cadets wore a Montana peak campaign hat and black leather leggings. The Negro Cavalrymen were stationed at West Point for a considerable period.

In Deference to Modern War

The coming of the magazine rifle had its influence on the cadet uniform, as we have seen. Quick firing artillery, motor vehicles, aircraft and the other devices of modern war have, in turn, exerted their influence. Modern technology has had a way of increasing the types of uniform required, as well as the number of garments of each type. Yet the same conditions have also made uniforms easier to obtain and to care for. Where two types of uniform sufficed in the early 1800's, seven or more are needed today; where a cadet might own two pairs of white trousers when he had to wash them himself, he can easily manage a dozen pairs with a steam laundry behind him.

When we entered the First World War in April 1917, cadet instruction was speeded up so that the Class of 1917 graduated two months ahead of time. The lower classes were pushed even faster, and as a result what was to have been the Class of 1921 left West Point in the fall of 1918. The Armistice, on 11 November of that year, and the return in December of the last class to graduate, for an additional six months of training at the Point, led to a chaotic medley of uniforms. The First Class, already commissioned officers, were uniformed as such in OD wool. The cadets of the next class had been issued grays and were the only ones to look like cadets. The Plebes who had entered in November 1918 wore OD enlisted men's clothing, distinguished only by an orange hat band (they were called "the Orioles" ever after). Not until June 1919 was the confusion ended.

In these cadet uniforms of 1914, we see that chevrons and service stripes are now worn on the overcoat; the Montana peak campaign hat has been replaced by a creased one again, and a new all white uniform has been introduced. Also we see the 1910 model Infantry equipment.

(Above) Plebes taking the oath of allegiance in 1913. The oath is always taken in the presence of the Corps Colors. The new cadets wear gray flannel shirts and dress trousers. The cadets in Dress Gray over white in the right foreground are upperclassmen charged with greeting the Plebes on arrival at West Point—the "New Cadet Detail."

(Below) All of these men are West Point cadets at the Graduation in June 1919. Those in olive drab had already been commissioned as officers when they returned to West Point at the end of the First World War for further study. This "Student Officer" class was the only one to wear an Army officer's uniform at West Point.

The field service uniform, about 1911, with the Model 1910 Infantry equipment — the notorious "long pack" which lasted into the Second World War. The clip-fed 1903 Springfield rifle required the pouch-type cartridge belt seen here.

The First World War did not exert too profound an effect on the cadet uniform, but it led to many changes in cadet life. The Corps began to work with the new weapons developed during the four years of fighting in Europe, and it was at once obvious that the West Point reservation was far from being large enough. Some field training had to be held at other Army posts. But for such work cadets continued to wear the gray field service uniform, with black leather leggings or, later, leather boots laced up the front. The campaign hat, since at least 1916, had been the regulation OD model, and the web equipment the same as worn by the Army.

By the 1930's the character of material had changed to such an extent that cadets were ruining their field service clothing with tears, grease and mud. The new kind of weapons required a tough, washable garment, and in 1938 a gray, one-piece coverall was issued for fatigue. It had a narrow

The Long Gray Line stands at rigid attention in this historic photo of 1917, taken when Marshal Joffre of France inspected the Corps on the Plain.

black stripe down the side and usually, the cadet's name stencilled on the back. Cadet gray thus entered the age of mechanization.

The general mobilization which preceded the Second World War rendered the procurement of the specialized West Point uniform very difficult and, in the case of some items, impossible. It would have been simple for the West Point authorities to have suspended cadet gray for the duration. It is to their great credit that they did not do so; they bent every effort to make sure that the cadets of the accellerated wartime classes saw as much of the traditional gray, black and gold as possible. Every class graduated in gray uniforms, even though the cadets had to wear overcoats for the winter commencements.

The years 1940-1942 brought many changes. The Corps received its first steel helmets (both old and new styles) and at the same time experimented with plastic summer helmets. Gray "overseas" caps came in to supplement for a time the dress cap. M-1 rifles replaced the Springfields in 1940.

Perhaps the most significant change, because it was permanent, was the adoption of the khaki shirt

Cadet uniform combinations in 1923. The types were quite similar to those of the present day but there were fewer uniforms with which to work.

Operating a heavy machine gun in 1942. The cadets wear gray coveralls. The tags on their helmet liners show their temporary ranks for the maneuver.

and trousers for summer drill. It was the same comfortable clothing worn throughout the Army, but it was nonetheless the khaki that West Point had shied away from for a half century. With it the cadet wore the black web belt and tie he had used with his gray field service uniform and, at first, a khaki "overseas" cap. The khaki uniform thereupon replaced the gray field service kit.

An unusual change came in 1942 when pilot-training was introduced at West Point. Nearby Stewart Field was expanded to take care of the "air cadets" who were preparing for the Army Air Corps. This training called for a different set of clothing, the most important being the flying helmet, sheepskin lined leather jacket, and gloves. In time, however, the terrain and weather around West Point was found not to be suitable for this training, and it was decided that the cadet's day was busy

Field training during World War II. The cadets are crossing a Bailey bridge. One mark of a good soldier is his ability to dress as efficiently for field service as he dresses smartly for parade. The cadets here are in their green HBT fatigues.

Field training with a howitzer in 1942. Here two cadets are wearing black sweaters in addition to gray coveralls. All carry gas masks.

enough without it. So June of 1946 saw the last cadets receive "wings" at graduation.

Another, and entirely novel uniform issued during the Second World War was for skiing. Slopes had been cut out of the hills behind the post and there cadets trained in winter for the type of mountain fighting many believed we would be required to undertake. As it turned out, no American soldier ever used skiis in combat, but the training opened up a new and exciting form of sport for many a cadet.

The end of the war saw the end of some of these

Third Classmen receiving instruction in signalling, 1951. Note that they wear nameplates (a common practice). The Corps insignia on their olive green helmet liners is the same as is worn on their gray caps.

Plebes in bivouac with pup tents in 1951. The U.S.M.A. shoulder sleeve insignia is seen on the left arm of the green fatigue uniform.

new uniforms and the start of others. Scarcely a year has passed since then which has not witnessed an important addition to the cadet's wardrobe. Today, in the summer, the cadet wears his khaki drill uniform with either a cap or a helmet liner (a new black satin scarf has just been added), or a green fatigue uniform that resembles the HBT (herring-bone twill) of World War II in color but not in fabric. New cadet details and others at the Academy put on gray at various times but, by and large, in summer, standard Army colors have taken over.

This picture of the cadet uniforms of 1944 includes several types adopted during the Second World War which have since been discarded: the khaki and gray garrison (overseas) caps, the shoulder tabs on the khaki shirt and the pilot's outfit.

"We Serve the Corps"

The military duties at West Point in support of the Military Academy have never been performed by cadets. Today they are handled by the 1802d Special Regiment (named for the year of West Point's founding), a complex team of 1200 specialists required to garrison and guard the post, to operate its utilities, and to assist in the practical instruction of the Corps of Cadets. The development of this large Regiment out of the little Regiment of Artillerists who garrisoned West Point in 1802 follows the corresponding growth of the Corps and demonstrates the almost incredible complexity of modern war.

By 1812, the Artillerist service troops were replaced by the Company of Bombardiers, Sappers and Miners — Engineer soldiers commonly known as the "Bombardiers." Between the Corps and Bombardiers a fierce rivalry existed, which now and then broke out into fist fights. It was the Company of Bombardiers which marched to the Niagara frontier when a British invasion threatened in 1814, and whose commander, Lt. Col. Eleazer Wood died in a fight near Fort Erie. When the Bombardiers returned, they helped build a monument to him on the Plain of West Point.

When the Bombardiers were disbanded in 1821, for eight years one or another company of Regular Artillery garrisoned West Point. However, in 1829, the Superintendent was authorized to form a special U.S.M.A. Detachment of Artillery, and ever since the Academy has had its own separate troops stationed on the post.

Unlike the West Point Band, whose uniform has usually been very different from other bands in the country, the various West Point detachments down to the 1802d Regiment have by and large worn the regulation Army uniform. After 1907 many of these were given special insignia instead of a regimental number. This was not a general practice, until the Regiment was activated in 1946 to contain

The first Cavalrymen arrived at the Military Academy in 1839 and the last ones left in 1947. This Regular Army Dragoon Detachment is seen filing past the West Point Hotel in 1852, in a wood engraving from *Gleason's Pictorial.*

WEST POINT BAND AND FIELD MUSIC, 1872

The drum major's bearskin hat with its tall plume stands high for all to admire. The officers of the Band today share with officers of the Corps the unique distinction of wearing the sword.

(Above) West Point faculty members and Tactical Officers, from six different branches of the service, about 1886. All wear undress uniforms.

(Right) Private Goetz of the Military Academy Detachment, riding on the box of this sleigh about 1895, is serving as the interpreter for a visiting dignitary, one of the duties in those days.

The first "radio car." In this Stanley Steamer, the West Point Artillery Detachment performed a successful experiment with wireless operation in 1910.

(Below) Officers and an enlisted woman of the Women's Army Corps (WAC) detachment stationed at West Point, 1954. The former are in the special white summer uniform. The WAC provides trained personnel for the Army Hospital at the Academy.

and administer the different detachments. At that time it was given a distinctive insignia and a set of colors. The men and women of the 1802d wear this insignia (a portcullis and book on a silver shield, with the motto: *"Nous servons le Corps"*) plus, in common with all military personnel on the post except cadets, a cloth shoulder sleeve insignia showing a blue helmet on a white field, piped with red.

The 1802d Regiment contains a detachment of the Women's Army Corps which provides trained personnel for the Army Hospital at West Point. Serving also at the Hospital, but not a part of the Regiment, are the Surgeons and the Army Nurses, all officers, who look after the health of the cadets and the other personnel stationed at West Point.

Distinct from the 1802d is the teaching staff of the Military Academy, in the main composed of officers detailed from the Army (and, since 1946, from the Air Force), along with some civilians. Heading this group are the Permanent Professors who wear their Army uniforms. In place of a branch insignia, on their sleeves they wear the coat of arms of the Military Academy. This same device is worn by the Directors of Physical Education, and by all civilian instructors. The civilians, inci-

Cadets, in green fatigue clothing, learn about infantry weapons from soldiers of the Combat Arms Detachment.

dentally, habitually wear the regulation Army officer's uniform but without insignia of rank.

Officers of the teaching staff have, with a few exceptions, always worn the uniform of their branch. For the first half century Engineer dress predominated, but thereafter the uniforms of all the branches of the Army could be seen. Now, while stationed at West Point, officers add the cloth West Point shoulder sleeve insignia, mentioned above, and a blue shield with the head of Pallas Athene, similar to the device worn on the shirt by cadets except as to color.

The Superintendent inspects his Infantry Honor Guard, part of the 1802d Special Regiment, 1954.

Black Knights of the Hudson

and Other Teams

Today, every cadet participates actively in at least sixteen different sports. Each afternoon during the academic year sees dozens of company teams playing tennis, lacrosse, hockey, baseball, and other sports in season. All of this is in addition to the regular varsity sports with their intercollegiate competition.

Every cadet must play on some intramural team every year — and on a team representing a different sport during *each* of his four years. It was while Superintendent of the Academy that Douglas Mac-Arthur intensified the system of compulsory intramural athletics — as one more means of training the cadets for leadership. His motto, inscribed on the walls of the gymnasium at West Point stresses the importance of this kind of training — as demonstrated by our men on the battlefields.

"Upon the fields of friendly strife
Are sown the seeds that,
Upon other fields, on other days,
Will bear the fruits of victory."

Moreover, cadets receive special instruction as coaches and sports organizers in their final year. The phrase "every man an athlete" is more than a motto.

When these West Point cadets played baseball for the U.S.M.A. in 1879, they played in their cadet uniforms. None of the Academy teams had special sports uniforms until a decade later.

This is not a scene from an old Charlie Chaplin movie, but a scrimmage in the Army-Navy game of 1891, the second ever played. Here for the first time we see West Pointers in special sports uniforms. The man in the derby is the referee.

Although the history of West Point's program of scientific physical training is one of gradual growth, at no time in the history of the Academy were cadets without opportunity for exercises and sports of some sort. In the earliest times, the daily chores of carrying water and chopping wood, coupled with strenuous military drill, were enough to keep a cadet in shape. Even so, as early as 1802, we read of the men hurrying off to "field sports" after classes were over. Later, in the 1840's, there was riding, fencing and even a game called "football"; and skating on the Hudson was a favorite sport in winter.

Since the fit of the cadet uniform was loosened at that time to allow greater freedom in playing these sports, we can be sure that cadets took part in their regular uniforms. This may seem strange, but it should be remembered that only since the turn of the century did men and women generally begin to wear truly light and simple clothing for sports.

Horseback riding as an exercise brought a special uniform for that purpose, but distinctive sport clothing, as we know it today, was not seen until 1890. In that year, acting on a challenge from the Naval Academy, West Point hastily formed a football team. Since it was necessary to distinguish the Army players from their opponents, a special football uniform was adopted: white turtle-neck sweaters marked with "USMA," football trousers with black socks, and striped stocking caps.

In the year 1885, West Point hired a head for the physical education program, called Master of the Sword; and its choice of the man was an excellent one. He was a civilian, Herman J. Koehler, and proved to be an experienced physical trainer and an immensely competent man as well. Before long all cadets were receiving instruction in fencing, swimming and gymnastics. From this start came the all-embracing program of physical education and intramural (cadets call it "intramurder") athletics. The colorful title, Master of the Sword, was changed to Director of Physical Education in August 1947.

In the past half century football has increased steadily in popularity at West Point, especially among graduates, just as it has at other colleges. The Military Academy has produced undefeated football teams on eight occasions between 1914 and 1949, and from 1944 to 1947 the cadets piled

(Above) The fencing team of about 1900 wears special fencing uniforms. The cadets on the right have on black sweaters and gray gym trousers. The Master of the Sword is seated toward the right.

(Left) Plebes getting tennis instruction. They wear gray trousers with white belts called "Plebeskins."

(Above) Members of the Varsity Hockey Squad in 1955 wearing golden jerseys.

(Right) In the intramural boxing ring, the fighter on the left is wearing "Plebe-skins" and the one on the right, regulation black gym trunks.

Every year the football schedule is climaxed by the Army-Navy game. This rivalry has continued since 1890 and today the game matches any other in the country for attendance and interest. The Army-Navy game is equally remarkable for the extent and ingenuity of the stunts carried out by cadets and midshipmen before the game and during the mid-period; almost anything can be expected from plastering a campus with leaflets from the air to theft of the Navy's goat. At this game the two great corps march onto the field and salute each side in turn before they take their places in the cheering section.

The present day sports uniforms, in style, are the same as worn in other colleges; the color scheme is always black, gold and gray. There are, however, a few distinctive features worth noting.

In 1941, Coach Earl H. Blaik introduced a plastic football helmet, golden in color. It is lighter

One of the "Black Knights of the Hudson" in his golden plastic helmet and football uniform. His pants are also golden and his jersey is black. From his number we can tell he is a half-back.

West Point's famous head football coach, Colonel Earl H. Blaik, prefers to wear this mixture of football and baseball gear as he watches his squad at practice.

up a remarkable record of thirty-two straight games without defeat. Army teams won the national championships of 1944 and 1945 and have, for many years, been among the top teams of the East.

Some of the Army's most distinguished officers have won a major "A" in football, and among these is President Dwight D. Eisenhower. A large share of this success in football is due to Colonel Earl H. Blaik who, after working with college sports for over 35 years, first as a player and later as coach and administrator, has won recognition among sports writers as one of the great coaches of modern football.

FOOTBALL UNIFORM AND LONG OVERCOAT OF WEST POINT CADETS, 1953

Victorious in the Army-Navy game, these "Black Knights of the Hudson" are carried off the field by their fellow cadets. In the intercollegiate number assignment system, "34" is a fullback and "81" an end.

and gives more protection than the leather type. The varsity jersey is black and the pants golden.

Numbers are given players to accord with their positions: 10's are quarterbacks, 20's and 40's halfbacks, 30's fullbacks, 50's centers, 60's guards, 70's tackles, and 80's ends.

What to call the West Point teams has often presented a problem. Early in the history of intercollegiate football the Academy eleven came to be called the "Army" team, especially in connection with the Army-Navy game. The varsity letter became the "A." But as other branches and posts of the Army developed their own teams of one sort or another, it became obvious that the Military Academy should not monopolize the name. Today, therefore, West Point athletic uniforms are never marked with "Army"; the old title survives only in the "A" and in news accounts of the games. Sports reporters poetically refer to the football team as "the Black Knights of the Hudson."

As at other colleges, athletic insignia is keenly sought after and proudly worn. Top honor is the "A," usually earned in major sports, and by any cadet making an Olympic team or breaking an intercollegiate record. There is a minor "A," awarded for minor sports. A cadet who has received an "A" in more than one sport is given a Gold Star to place on it for each additional sport. There is also a Navy Gold Star awarded for participating in a victorious game against the Naval Academy.

Other athletic insignia include the Academy Monogram, presented to outstanding athletes who have not won an "A"; Class Numerals, presented to Fourth Classmen on Corps squads for participation in Plebe games, and the various types of the "A" awarded managers, cheerleaders and muleriders. The letters, monograms and numerals awarded players are gray on black; the major and minor letters won by managers are black on gray, while the cheerleaders' "A" is gold on black. Each year three muleriders (who have actually ridden one of the Army mules) wins a gold "A" on a white pullover sweater.

The letters and other devices were first worn on all black sweaters which buttoned down the front. In the 1930's gold and gray stripes were added to the sweater cuffs. They were worn during study hours, at athletic formation, and at recreation; and

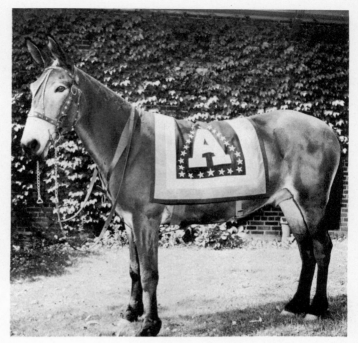

The Army Mule has been the mascot of West Point football teams for more than 50 years but no one knows just why the mule was chosen. Plebes compete for the honor of riding the mules and the successful muleriders are awarded an "A." This is "Bud," one of the mules in 1954. A current "mule" is an Ecuadorean burro named "Pancho."

the earlier ones were incredibly warm. Within recent years the sweater has been replaced by a gray jacket and a black, hooded parka — and another landmark disappeared from West Point.

Selection of cheerleaders is made by cadets themselves. The Cheer Leader Squad consists of twenty men and includes muleriders and the cadets in charge of the various stunts carried on during mid-periods of games. Fourth Classmen try out for the Squad and are judged on the basis of voice, imagination and that particular kind of infectious enthusiasm that gets good cheers. Muleriders, on the other hand, are selected from among the Plebes who know how to ride, a qualification growing rarer with each year.

For more than fifty years the mule has been the mascot of West Point football teams. The origin of the practice is not clear except that, around 1900, mules were faithful if not always lovable helpmates of the American soldier in combat and seemed to represent the tough characteristics expected of Army teams. Incidentally, one of the current "mules" is actually an Ecuadorian burro named Pancho.

The Cadet's Day

A cadet's typical day is long, busy and precisely regulated. Every minute of it is spent in a uniform of some sort. It has always been this way. In June 1842, William Dutton, a Plebe just arrived at West Point, tried to describe the life to his brother: ". . . We have five in our room, which you know is but about 10 by 12. At 5 A.M. which is ½ an hour after the morning gun, the drums are beat by the barracks, & the cry grows —— 'fall in there,' when we all have to be in the ranks or be reported. The roll is then called, we go to our rooms & have 15 minutes to roll up our blankets, put them up, wash, clean the room, etc., when *every thing must* be in order. We have no matresses & only 2 blankets to lay on the floor and cover ourselves with, & when

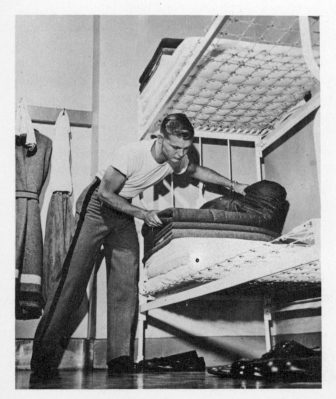

we all five spread ourselves out we just cover the floor ——

"We then remain in our rooms until the drums beat for breakfast, again if missing we are reported. We then march to the mess hall, & if one speaks, raises his hand, looks to the right or left (which is the case on all parade) we are reported; indeed we are reported for everything. I have been so fortunate as to escape as yet. When we arrive at the tables, the command is given 'take seats,' & then such a scrambling you never saw. For breakfast we have the remains of the meat of the former day's dinner, cut up with potato and considerable gravy — & not more than two thirds of them get a bit — bread cut in chunks, butter and coffee. We have to eat as fast as we can, & before we get enough, the command is given 'Squad rise.'

"At dinner we have 'Roast Beef,' & boiled potato, & bread — no butter, at Tea, bread & butter & tea. We have to drill twice a day, & a good many faint away. It is *terrible,* but I like the whole of it. After we have marched from tea, we stay in our room till ½ hour past 9 when we can go to bed if we choose, & at taps at 10 every light must be out & after that the inspector happens in all times of night."

This was in 1842. It is a far cry from today's ample menus, modern barracks, and fine facilities for recreation and training. But in precision of formations and duties, the Academy has not greatly changed.

First Call for reveille is blown by a detail of Hell Cats, the musicians of the enlisted band and field

Cadets are allowed 20 minutes for policing their barracks rooms. After this, they assemble for breakfast at 6:30. The cadet here is wearing the regulation undershirt and we can see his woolen regulation bathrobe hanging on the wall.

(Above) Between classes we get a glimpse of the cadets in their classroom attire, wearing gray jackets and one with his varsity "A." The men standing braced are Plebes.

(Below) These cadets are showing their short overcoats, gray scarfs and winter gloves — a regulation uniform for winter, 1954. The two stripes on their cuffs denote that they are Second Classmen.

music, at 5:50 in the morning, and ten minutes later comes Assembly. All cadets must stand this first formation in Dress Gray. There follows about twenty minutes for the police of barracks prior to assembly for breakfast at 6:30, in the same uniform. Here, as at all formations, overcoats, raincoats or other garments are added as the weather and the uniform signal flags dictate. (These can be seen from all the cadets' rooms.) After breakfast comes a study period until assembly for the first class at 7:55. Cadets attend this formation in gray shirts or in some other uniform suitable to the work to be done. Laboratory work, for instance, usually is performed in fatigue uniform.

Most men have two classes in the morning. By noon they must be back in barracks and in the prescribed Dress Gray for dinner, assembly for which comes at 12:10. The Corps is played into dinner by the fifes and drums. The meal lasts at least a half hour, during which the two senior classes can leave at will. The other cadets quit the mess after the command, "Battalions Rise."

At 1:00 p.m. the bugle blows assembly for the first afternoon class, and for the second one at

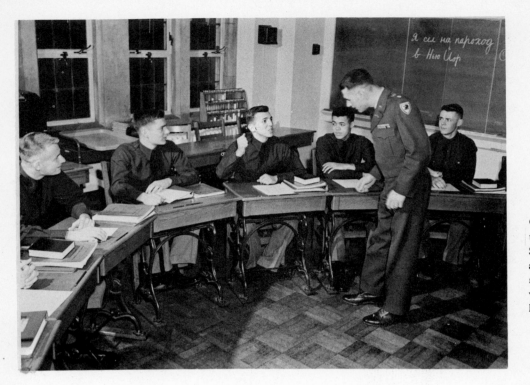

One of the foreign languages taught at West Point is Russian. Small classes permit individual attention to each student. The men here are Plebes and hence wear no collar ornaments. They have on their dark gray shirts.

2:15. Cadets normally have only one class each afternoon, but the extra time is usually spent in drill and tactical instruction. This calls for either the gray shirt or the fatigue uniform, under arms.

The intramural athletic program commences at 3:30 for everyone and lasts at least one hour. For athletics a different uniform is worn for every sport, and the varicolored jerseys used to distinguish teams add an even greater array of colors. Showered and dressed again in Dress Gray, the cadet may have about a half hour of relatively free time. On some days during this brief period, however, those who have demerits form under arms in the central area and walk them off.

It is unusual for the Corps to stand Retreat on weekdays. On Saturdays, however, there is a parade formation of some sort at 1:10. If the weather is fine and the ground on the Plain hard, it may be a Full Dress affair. In winter it is usually a "bandbox" review in the central area. But whatever the formation, it is invariably followed by an inspection. This over — and all the rifles, swords and accouterments returned to quarters — the cadet is allowed to relax a bit until Monday morning.

The Corps, on a weekday, falls in for supper at 6:20. Call to Quarters follows at 7:15 and cadets must go to their rooms to study until Taps is blown at 10:15, which means lights out for all except a few with special permissions. "Late lights" are doused at 11:00 to the taps of a drum ("Late Taps") and the Military Academy, in theory at least, sleeps.

In his room, even as outside, the cadet is in uniform, since every article he owns from slippers to bathrobe is regulated. For years there has been a uniform bathrobe, and today there are two. The winter robe is of gray cotton blanket cloth, piped with black, and with broad gold and black stripes on sleeves and around the bottom. The summer "beachrobe" is a bluish cotton robe with gray and gold piping.

Even in bed the cadet is clothed in gray, for his pajamas are of this color, piped with black and gold. Except for his underwear, which is entirely white, some combination of Military Academy colors is used on all clothing, from swimming trunks to waist belts.

Speaking of underwear, an interesting item was worn by several generations of cadets, and not discontinued for sale at the Cadet Store until 1945: the long cotton drawers called "Scrivens." These were once manufactured by a firm named James A. Scriven & Co. in Long Island City, N.Y., which went out of business in 1917. So attached was the Academy to these long drawers that the authorities arranged to have them made for twenty-eight years

WEST POINT PLEBES IN CLASS UNIFORM AND UPPERCLASSMEN IN JACKETS, 1954

The Plebes must march to class "braced." The cadet with the "A" on his jacket has earned this top honor in a major sport.

The gold star was awarded for participating in a victorious game against the Naval Academy. The cadet Officer of the Day stands in the doorway.

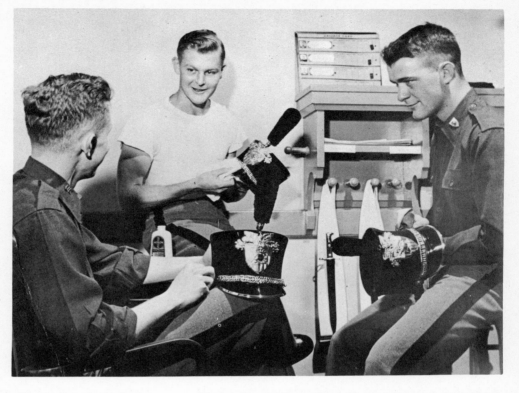

An occupation that can easily take a half hour is polishing the "tarbucket" hat before a parade. Note the class shield and the "U.S." on the cadets' collars; a cadet officer wears his rank insignia in place of the "U.S."

longer. The name, "Scrivens," continued to designate the drawers and remained an important word in the cadet vocabulary. Even today it fills older graduates with nostalgia.

Dress Gray over white is a regulation parade dress for summertime. The equipment is identical with that worn for Full Dress. This parade on the Plain took place about 1950.

Returning to the schedule, Sundays and holidays provide a different order of events and hence uniforms. Chapel, for example, is attended usually in full dress coat, white or gray trousers, and gray or white dress cap; cadet officers wear their sashes and swords and others their white waist belts. Should a cadet visit the Hotel Thayer after dinner

First and foremost, West Point is a college and the cadets are students. Their everyday uniforms are designed to give them the maximum of comfort.

he would wear the All White uniform (in summer), or the Full Dress as for chapel, but without belts. Should he go instead to the movies, he would be in Dress Gray only. White gloves are worn to chapel and hops, but not to the Thayer.

Cadet Regulations list 80 activities a cadet could conceivably participate in, with the uniform for each. They range everywhere from "escorting while in hospital" to "funerals," "organ recitals," and "skiing." Uniforms for special events of this sort, attended by only a few cadets, cannot be indicated by the flags and hence the long list is required.

Why couldn't the choice of the appropriate uniform for, let's say, attendance at the Model Airplane Club or acting as best man at a wedding, be left to the discretion of the cadet? In 90 per cent of the cases it safely could, and in practice often is. But with all the possible combinations to select from, it saves the cadet a lot of time if he knows ahead what to wear, and it insures the uniformity essential to a military operation of any sort.

At the end of this book you will find a description of the sixteen uniform combinations worn by cadets today. Boiled down, they come to five basic

uniforms: gray Full Dress and all that goes with it, Dress Gray with the gray shirt as an alternate, All White for formal occasions in summer, khaki for work in summer, and green fatigues for the rougher sorts of job.

This shows the proper way the cape must be folded back and the sash tied when a long overcoat is worn. This cadet officer is talking with a British field marshal who is visiting the Academy.

Parades, Dances and Graduations

When most of us think of cadet gray we think of Full Dress. Although the cadet full dress uniform (what the cadet calls FD), with its bullet buttons, white belts, glittering brass plates, and tarbucket, is worn only for special ceremonies, it is, after all, the traditional uniform of West Point.

What is the exact color of cadet gray today? It probably began as a charcoal shade, acquired a bluish tint early in its history, and now tends toward the purple. For a time before the Civil War (as well as afterward), the cloth came from the Charlottesville (Virginia) Woolen Mills. In 1861 this supply was cut off (as in 1813), and cloth suddenly became difficult to obtain from any source. Uniforms had to be patched and re-used. One cadet of the Civil War recalls the especially fanciful patches his classmates wore on the seats of their trousers.

The Charlottesville Mills finally failed in the 1930's and had to be taken over by its creditors. The story goes that the original owners took with them the secret of the dye that guaranteed uniformity, and that the shade of gray has never been constant since that time. True or not, today West Point tailors cut a single uniform from the same piece of cloth, to be certain the coat and trousers will match. Not only can one bolt differ in shade from another, but one end of a single bolt can vary from the other end.

In 1923, as we have said, the Fried Egg on the hat had its devices changed to face *dexter* instead of *sinister,* and all over the Academy the same change took place. Only the granite and bronze

A favorite spot to take "drags" is this Battle Monument on the Plain. Around the globe are the names of Regulars killed in action during the Civil War.

The cadet uniform combinations of 1955. The dress of cadet officers and the numerous athletic uniforms are not shown in this photo.

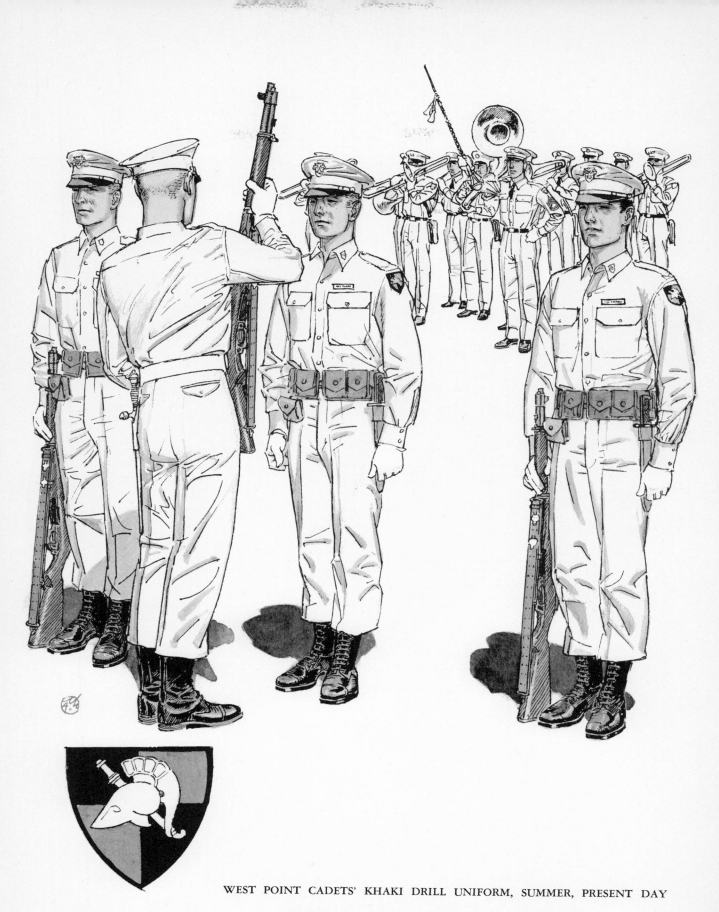

WEST POINT CADETS' KHAKI DRILL UNIFORM, SUMMER, PRESENT DAY

Khaki was first adopted at the Military Academy during the
Second World War, and is the uniform principally worn during
the summer.

The Color Party and Corps Colors on parade on the Plain, 1955. The first four men are Color Sergeants; bringing up the rear are two supply sergeants and two sergeants-major.

Guarding the entrance to Flirtation Walk is the Kelleher-Jobes Arch. This cadet in his Full Dress uniform with gray trousers is escorting his "drag" determinedly through the famous arch.

coats of arms on the buildings proved impractical of alteration and remains backwards today, in defiance of Heraldry.

Bullet or bell buttons, alas, have gone, although you would never know it from a casual glance. The buttons that, for over a century, had proved irresistible to "femmes" — so irresistible that cadets were forced to carry an extra supply to replace those snipped off — succumbed to modern efficiency. It was found that a button, rounded at one end only, fitted more snugly and still looked like the real thing. This style now adorns the full dress coat.

A favorite place for passing out buttons, as well as other favors, has for many, many decades been Flirtation Walk. This half-mile long path begins near Trophy Point and winds through delightful rustic scenery, along the edge of the Hudson. It is closed to all but cadets and their drags, and so should its story. Should the reader want to learn more about landmarks like Kissing Rock he must seek out some girl who has trod that romantic path while we return to our subject.

The full dress coat is, on special occasions in summer, worn with or without belts, in combination with a white cap and white trousers. This is the 50-50 uniform for hops and chapel, and it is the one worn for Graduation exercises. Special nylon silk gloves are worn at hops; and on these occasions it is the hop managers who wear red sashes, not necessarily the officers.

Hops are held today in several buildings at West Point, usually in the Gymnasium or in Cullum Hall. Informal dances are given at the Hotel Thayer, which is on the reservation, close by the South Gate. Until recent years, hops were most formal affairs at which cadets habitually wore Full Dress. Many are still formal but nowadays there are quite a few informal teas and costume hops, and there are also square dances.

All the four classes hold hops, often together, although Fourth Classmen have to wait until Christ-

mas for their first dance. West Point is fairly unique in that cadets still use hop cards, which are filled ahead of time after much arranging. Of late the trend has been toward reserving one's own drag for more and more numbers; apparently the desire to dance with the same girl is stronger now than in our father's generation. Another modern note is the juke box in the Weapons Room which, when girls are there, is kept running continuously for informal dancing.

No matter what or where the dance is, it is always colorful and gay. Only the final number, "Army Blue," brings that traditional note of sadness which is so unforgettable a part of a West Point hop. For with every final number comes the unspoken thought that ahead in Army life may lie

Cadet "hops" have always been splendid affairs as we can see by this 1898 drawing by Howard Chandler Christy. Then, as now, the uniform for after-supper hops in winter was Full Dress Gray. Hop cards are still in use at West Point. There are a good many informal and costume hops, as well as square dances today. (From *Harper's Weekly*.)

even more heart-rending farewells. Every cadet hop, alas, has about it a suggestion of the Duchess of Richmond's ball before Waterloo.

The uniform for weddings at West Point — at least for the groom and usually the ushers — is khaki, for not until a man has graduated can he marry. Every June Week sees a spate of these weddings in one or another of the chapels. Amid flowers from the gardens on the reservation, to music by the chapel organs or perhaps a string quartette from the Band, and always under the traditional arch of swords, these new officers and their brides start off together on their careers in the Army or Air Force. All the equipment for a wedding is provided; the Cadet Chapel has to keep a supply of officers' swords and Sam Browne belts just for use at weddings, since the sword is no longer regulation in the land and air services.

This dazzling summer All White uniform is probably the least known of those worn by the Corps. Accouterments are the same as for Full Dress. The photograph above shows the first occasion on which the All White was worn in a street parade — up New York City's Fifth Avenue alongside Central Park, August 1952.

There is the so-called All White, with or without belts, which comprises a white coat, cap and trousers, and is also used in summer for chapel, hops and special ceremonies when ordered. Worn at West Point for over fifty years, it made its first appearance outside in a New York City street parade in 1952.

At the end of the West Point year comes June Week, a landmark for every cadet, when his position, privileges and responsibilities change. For the First Classman there is Graduation, followed by a new sort of life, and, possibly marriage. For the

WEST POINT CADET GRADUATION UNIFORM, 1955

When the last cadet has received his diploma, and the First Captain has given the command, "Class Dismissed," the graduating class flings its white caps high in the air—proof that its days with cadet gray are over.

Plebe there is Recognition and the end of the restrictions of his first year. And for all there is a one-month furlough.

June Week sees hundreds of graduates back for class reunions. There are several parades and reviews but the most impressive is Graduation Parade. Every move made is inspired by tradition, and even the music played — tunes like "The Dashing White Sergeant" and "Army Blue" — form an unchanging part of the ceremony. At a point in the parade the class about to graduate falls out of ranks and forms a long reviewing line on the side of the Plain. Before this line the Corps marches by in salute, which the First Classmen return by removing their hats.

Immediately after this parade the Plebes are recognized by the upperclassmen, and that night comes the Graduation Hop. Graduation exercises follow the next morning in a solemn and impressive

Parading from the Central Area is this cadet company in "50-50" Full Dress. Leading is the company commander, a captain. Behind him march the right guide (corporal), first sergeant, and guidon corporal. In this picture we can see the perfect rhythm and timing of the cadets on parade, a preciseness that distinguishes West Point men.

ceremony. When the last cadet has received his diploma there is a brief exchange of the "Long Corps Yell" between the classes and then the First Captain gives "Class Dismissed." With that the white caps of the graduating class are flung high in the air as proof that their days with cadet gray are over.

Army Blue, Army Blue,
  Hurrah for Army Blue,
We'll bid farewell to Kaydet Gray,
  And don the Army Blue.

Appendix A —
Authorized Uniforms 1955

Drill A: Gray worsted shirt, black tie, gray trousers, black belt, dress cap, dress shoes, black socks, garters, arms and equipment as ordered.

Drill B: Fatigue jacket, fatigue trousers, black belt, combat boots, cushion sole socks, helmet liner.

Drill C: Khaki shirt, black tie, khaki trousers, black belt, khaki dress cap, dress shoes, black socks, garters.

Drill D: Khaki shirt, khaki trousers, black belt, combat boots, cushion sole socks, helmet liner, arms and equipment as ordered.

Dress Gray: Dress coat, gray trousers, suspenders, dress cap, dress shoes, black socks, garters.

Dress Gray over white: Dress coat, white trousers, suspenders, dress cap, dress shoes, black socks, garters.

Full Dress Gray: Full dress coat, gray trousers, suspenders, dress cap, dress shoes, black socks, garters. When worn under arms, substitute full dress hat (with plume for officers and acting officers and pompon for others) for dress cap.

Full Dress Gray over white: Full dress coat, white trousers, suspenders, dress cap (unless the white cap is prescribed), dress shoes, black socks, garters. When worn under arms, substitute full dress hat (with plume for officers and acting officers and pompon for others) for dress cap.

All White: White coat, white trousers, suspenders, white cap, dress shoes, black socks, garters.

Class: Gray worsted shirt, gray trousers, black tie, black belt, dress cap, dress shoes, black socks, garters. Gray gymnasium trousers may be substituted for dress gray trousers for informal wear in barracks after ami or for extra-curricular activities when authorized by the O-in-C of the activity.

Laboratory: Fatigue jacket, fatigue trousers, black belt, dress cap, dress shoes, black socks, garters, name card. Khaki cap will be substituted during the summer and modified summer period.

Golf: White sport shirt, khaki trousers, black gymnasium shoes, white socks, black belt.

CCQ (Summer): White sport shirt, white trousers, black tie, dress cap, black belts, black socks, garters, black shoes.

Gym A: Athletic shirt, gymnasium trousers, black belt, white wool socks, supporter, shoes as prescribed by the Director of Physical Education.

Gym B: Athletic shirt, athletic shorts, white wool socks, supporter, shoes as prescribed by the Director of Physical Education.

Ski: Gray worsted shirt, gray gymnasium trousers, white athletic or OD socks, ski boots, gray leather gloves or ski mittens. Parka, wool cap, gray jacket or black sweater are optional.

Appendix B —
Chronology of Events

16 March 1802. U.S.M.A. and Corps of Engineers established.

3 Dec. 1802. Distinctive uniform approved for officers of the Corps of Engineers.

30 April 1810. Distinctive uniform authorized for cadets.

2 May 1814. First regulations issued by War Department governing the cadet uniform.

Summer 1815. Captain Partridge introduced gray uniforms with leather caps; white belts worn for parade.

4 Sep. 1816. Secretary of War approved the gray uniform, but specified "round hats" instead of leather caps (round hats were worn for fatigue until 1825); gilt bullet buttons prescribed.

23 Sep. 1817. Chevrons first prescribed for cadet officers.

Fall 1818. Bell-crowned leather cap introduced.

15 Nov. 1818. New system of chevrons prescribed.

29 June 1819. First mention of "fatigue jacket and trousers" for summer (probably of unbleached cotton or linen; worn continuously until 1870).

During 1820. Pantaloons were lengthened and strapped under the instep.

11 Aug. 1821. First record of Corps Colors; two carried.

3 Sep. 1821. Wearing of all civilian clothes by cadets at West Point, except hats and overcoats, prohibited.

28 Oct. 1822. Cut of dress coat altered; braid hereafter worn straight rather than "herring-bone."

8 March 1823. Only cadet officers and NCO's authorized to wear gold cord and tassels on leather cap.

17 April 1823. White leather gloves prescribed.

29 April 1823. Coat collar altered "to fit the neck and hook in front," with shirt collar worn outside.

10 Sep. 1823. Cadet Assistant Professors authorized extra buttonholes and buttons on dress coat.

16 Oct. 1823. New pattern flintlock muskets (Model 1816) issued.

7 May 1824. New flintlock muskets with browned barrels issued.

22 April 1825. Cloth forage caps issued; wearing of civilian model hats at West Point prohibited.

29 Sep. 1825. Undress gray coatee and pantaloons without braid prescribed; worn until about 1828.

17 Feb. 1826. Hair ordered to be cut monthly.

14 July 1826. New pattern pompon issued.

7 Aug. 1826. Sashes directed to be tied on right hip.

20 June 1828. "Regulation fatigue jacket" provided.

6 Nov. 1828. Regulation single-breasted overcoat and cape, of gray cloth, prescribed and no other overcoat to be worn thereafter; flat gilt overcoat button with "CADET" prescribed.

29 June 1830. New insignia prescribed for cadet officers (essentially the type worn today).

11 May 1831. Cadet Musket, Model 1830, issued.

28 June 1831. Cross belts of white webbing replaced those of leather.

11 June 1832. Sashes ordered to be tied on left hip.

16 March 1834. Shirt collars not to be worn outside.

1 April 1834. Leather folding forage caps replaced the cloth model.

15 March 1835. White cotton gloves replaced leather gloves.

About 1835. First Class Ring adopted.

(By 1836). Austrian knot on gray pantaloons abolished.

10 June 1838. Stocks of black "bombasine" (cotton and silk mixed) replaced those of leather.

24 Nov. 1838. Wearing of vests made "optional," and for undress only.

22 May 1839. First model of cadet sword issued.

July 1839. Black beaver "stovepipe" dress cap, with Artillery crossed-cannon on front, replaced the bell-crowned cap.

14 Oct. 1839. Black leather saber belts ordered for wear by cadets when mounted.

18 Feb. 1840. Worsted pompons replaced feather pompons.

26 June 1840. New model belts with black leather frogs issued.

July 1840. Cloth forage caps replaced leather type.

30 June 1841. Cadet officers issued white leather shoulder belts in place of waist belts; ordered to wear sashes around waist whenever sword is worn.

1 Sep. 1841. New pattern bayonet frogs issued.

About 1841. Stand of Corps Colors reduced to single flag.

11 May 1842. Cadet officers given black cock's feather plumes and Engineer castles to replace crossed cannon.

29 April 1843. Shirt collars to be worn outside as part of the uniform.

5 July 1843. Engineer castles replaced crossed cannon on all caps.

25 May 1844. Instep straps on all pantaloons (except those used for riding) removed.

24 March 1845. New pattern percussion Cadet Muskets, Model 1841, issued; cap pouches issued.

28 Aug. 1845. Fly front pants replaced those with fall fronts.

30 Nov. 1847. Cadet Assistant Professors authorized to wear captain's chevrons with star (probably instead of extra buttons).

27 March 1848. Cadets on leave authorized to wear blue frock coats without insignia of rank; a dark blue "furlough cap" was worn with this uniform.

August 1848. Oilcloth cap covers issued.

9 Aug. 1849. First India rubber capes issued.

22 Oct. 1849. Gray cloth riding jacket and pants issued (subsequently a similar jacket made of gray flannel was adopted for fatigue).

3 Sep. 1850. Extra braid and buttons on full dress coat authorized for Cadet Assistant Professors (14 rows in all).

31 Oct. 1850. Buckskin gauntlets adopted for riding.

12 June 1851. Overcoat made double-breasted; design of flat gilt overcoat buttons altered to show eagle, "CADET," and "U.S.M.A." Summer fatigue jackets prescribed as being of "brown" linen drilling.

29 June 1852. Low collars, open in front, introduced.

Summer 1853. New model dress cap introduced (no change in insignia).

During 1861. "Chasseur" model blue forage cap introduced.

During 1862. Collars altered to hook up in front.

Overcoats and overshoes	Drill C	Drill D	Gray for Dress Gray

Red and Green

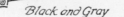

Black and Gray

Black and Gray

Gray, Yellow, White, Red, Black or Green

So that all the cadets will wear the proper uniform for each occasion, signal flags are flown in the barrack areas, and cadets can take a peek from their barrack room windows before dressing.

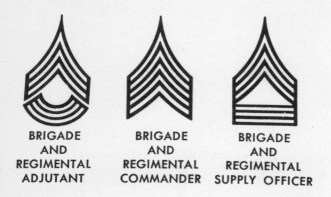

BRIGADE AND REGIMENTAL ADJUTANT

BRIGADE AND REGIMENTAL COMMANDER

BRIGADE AND REGIMENTAL SUPPLY OFFICER

BATTALION ADJUTANT

BATTALION COMMANDER

BATTALION SUPPLY OFFICER

CAPTAIN

BRIGADE AND REGIMENTAL TRAINING OFFICER

LIEUTENANT

REGIMENTAL SUPPLY SERGEANT

BATTALION TRAINING OFFICER

REGIMENTAL SERGEANT MAJOR

BATTALION SERGEANT MAJOR

FIRST SERGEANT

SUPPLY SERGEANT

COLOR SERGEANT (on upper sleeve)

SERGEANT (on upper sleeve) CORPORAL (on lower sleeve)

5 Dec. 1864. Chevrons for Military Merit, and Medals for Academic Merit, pre-scribed.

11 Aug. 1866. Chevrons for Military Merit, and Medals for Academic Merit, re-scinded.

12 Sep. 1866. Lower model dress cap approved (for about two years it had a small Engineer Corps castle and a brush-like pompon).

November 1867. New pattern breech-loading rifles issued (probably Model 1866).

During 1867. Forage cap device adopted.

Summer 1869. Sunburst design adopted for dress cap; worsted pompon readopted.

Early 1870. New pattern rifles issued (Cadet Model 1868, marked with cadets' names).

June 1870. White linen jacket and trousers issued, replacing brown linen fatigue jackets.

8 Oct. 1870. Uniform "dressing gown" authorized and civilian models prohibited (not consistently authorized).

About 1870. Corps Color became the Stars and Stripes.

During 1872. Second model of cadet sword adopted.

22 Dec. 1877. "White India helmet" authorized for summer fatigue duty.

During 1878. New dress cap and insignia adopted.

17 June 1881. Brass spike, chain and chinstrap authorized for white helmet for full dress.

23 Feb. 1884. Design of collar on full dress coat altered to present pattern.

About 1885. McKeever cartridge boxes introduced.

15 June 1889. Gray fatigue (now "Dress") coat introduced, replacing gray riding jacket and gray flannel (shell) jacket.

During 1889. Standing white collar replaced turned-down shirt collar.

29 Sep. 1893. Gray jersey trousers and brown canvas leggings introduced for riding.

May 1894. Corps Color authorized in addition to National Color.

Summer 1894. Gray "mackintosh" (rain coat) first issued.

During 1895. Krag-Jorgensen (Model 1892) magazine rifle received.

Summer 1898. Gray field service uniform (campaign hat, gray flannel shirt, black tie, and leggings) introduced, together with full field equipment and blanket roll (apparently replaced white linen fatigue uniform).

13 Oct. 1898. U.S.M.A. Coat of Arms adopted.

4 March 1899. Distinctive colors (black, gold, gray) adopted for U.S.M.A. athletic teams.

26 April 1899. New full dress cap authorized and cross belts revived (first worn together 3 July 1899).

24 Oct. 1899. Service stripes (one for each year at U.S.M.A.) adopted.

About 1900. Black ("shaker") sweater authorized.

July 1902. First use of gray Corps Color with U.S.M.A. Coat of Arms.

12 June 1903. Dress ("pill-box") cap issued to replace "chasseur" model fatigue cap; white summer helmet abolished.

During 1903. Montana peak replaces crease for campaign hats.

During 1905. Model 1903 rifles replaced Krag-Jorgensens.

About 1910. Chevrons and service stripes placed on overcoats; gray campaign hats with center crease readopted.

During 1911. Model 1910 Infantry equipment received.

15 Dec. 1913. All White dress summer uniform authorized.

During 1913. Star insignia on collar authorized for Distinguished Cadets.

About 1914. OD campaign hat with Montana peak issued; gray drill breeches issued.

During 1916. Uniform signal flags first used.

2 Nov. 1918. OD uniforms with yellow hatband and gray cuff stripe authorized for Fourth Class (replaced by grays in Spring 1919).

April 1920. Leather "cuff" leggings replaced canvas leggings for most formations (later replaced by black laced field boots).

November 1920. Black sweater made item of issue (colored stripes authorized 16 Jan. 1925).

2 July 1923. U.S.M.A. Coat of Arms changed.

During 1923. Third model of cadet sword adopted.

28 May 1926. Short gray overcoat authorized (not consistently worn).

3 May 1938. Gray coverall authorized.

August 1940. M-1 rifles replaced Model 1903.

Fall 1941. Collar insignia for Cadet Instructors authorized (discontinued after 1942).

Early 1942. Old pattern steel helmets issued.

11 March 1942. Gray garrison (overseas) cap approved.

31 March 1942. Army issue leggings adopted; color of coverall changed to dark gray; black laced shoe replaced by Army issue combat boot.

30 April 1942. Sun helmets and khaki drill uniform with garrison (overseas) cap authorized.

Cadet Chevrons today. The black lines represent the stripes that would be worn with the Dress Gray uniform and overcoat.

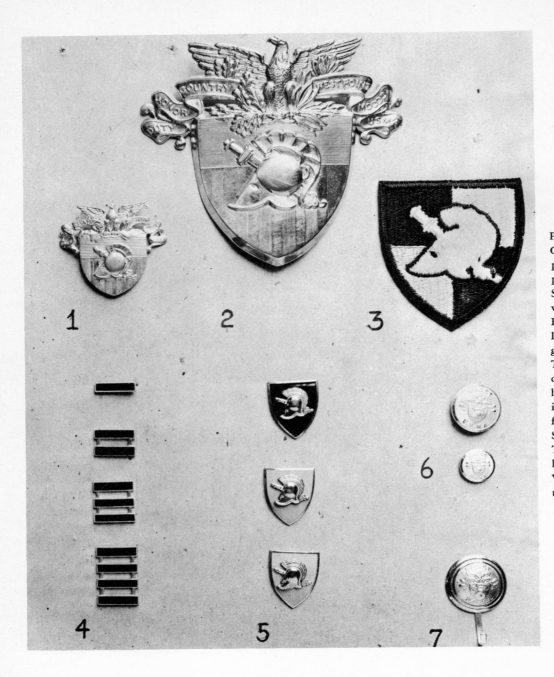

Present day insignia of the Corps of Cadets: 1. Brass plate for dress cap. 2. Brass plate for full dress hat. 3. Shoulder sleeve insignia for wear on issue clothing. 4. Rank insignia for shirt collars; from top: corporal, sergeant, lieutenant, and captain. There are five and six-bar devices for regimental and brigade commanders. 5. Class insignia for shirt collars, etc.; from top: First Class (black), Second Class (gray), and Third Class (gold). 6. Brass buttons for overcoats and All White uniforms. 7. Side button on full dress hats.

16 May 1942. U.S.C.C. distinctive insignia (black shield) approved.
3 June 1942. Campaign hat discontinued after issue to Class of 1946.
9 June 1942. New pattern steel helmets and liners ordered.
16 Sep. 1942. Black laced field boots discontinued.
9 Nov. 1942. Army issue field jacket adopted for summer training.
10 Nov. 1942. Riding breeches abolished; gray athletic trousers approved.
3 June 1943. Shoulder tabs approved to show class and rank on khaki drill uniform.
July 1945. New field pack, shelter half, and entrenching tool issued.
12 Feb. 1946. Green "Byrd cloth" fatigue uniform (trousers, cap and jacket) replaced gray coverall and gray garrison cap; short overcoat authorized.
July 1946. Gray gabardine jacket (windbreaker) authorized (issue suspended 1 July 1949).
Spring 1947. Dark gray (tropical worsted wool) tailored shirt replaced gray flannel shirt.

During 1947. Enamelled rank insignia introduced for shirt collars.
During 1949. Distinctive insignia first made in three colors (black, gray, gold) to distinguish three senior classes.
27 Nov. 1950. Web rifle sling authorized (for summer training only).
During 1950. U.S.C.C. shoulder sleeve insignia introduced for wear on Army issue clothing; zippers placed on dress coats; lace type combat boots first issued to some cadets.
7 March 1951. OD poncho replaced OD rubberized raincoat.
1 Sep. 1952. Black wool hooded parka and gray gabardine jacket substituted for black sweater. (Knitted cuffs were added to parka in fall of 1953.)
Spring 1953. Gray gym shorts and athletic T-shirts with crest first issued.
July 1953. Last issue of white gym belt.
June 1955. Black satin scarfs and black helmet liners (with gray stripe) adopted by First Class New Cadet Details for wear with khaki drill uniform.
During 1955. Lace type combat boot completely replaced clasp type.

DATE DUE

4/5 JAN 30			
APR 09			
GAYLORD			PRINTED IN U.S.A.

PIANO · VOCAL · GUITAR

P9-CBD-975

HIGH SCHOOL MUSICAL 2

CONTENTS

ISBN-13: 978-1-4234-3054-4
ISBN-10: 1-4234-3054-9

Walt Disney Music Company
Wonderland Music Company, Inc.

DISTRIBUTED BY

HAL·LEONARD®
CORPORATION
7777 W. BLUEMOUND RD. P.O. BOX 13819 MILWAUKEE, WI 53213

In Australia Contact:
Hal Leonard Australia Pty. Ltd.
4 Lentara Court
Cheltenham, Victoria, 3192 Australia
Email: ausadmin@halleonard.com

Visit Hal Leonard Online at
www.halleonard.com

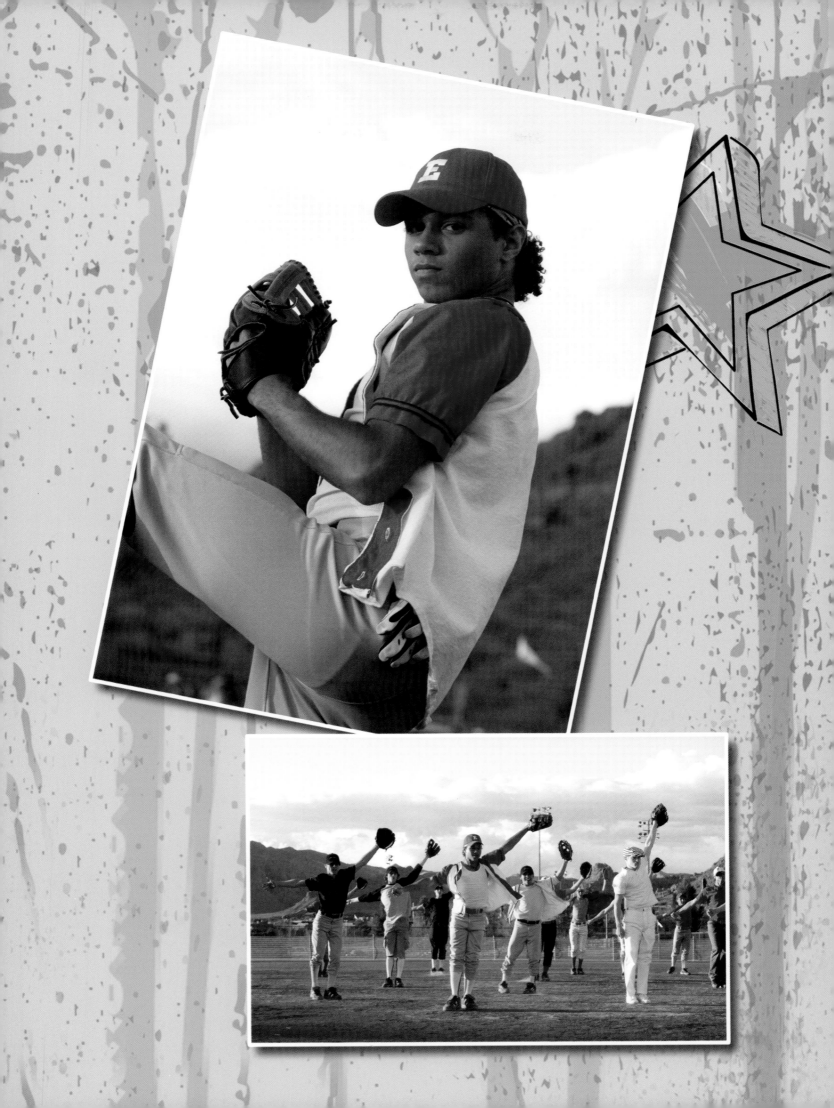

WHAT TIME IS IT

Words and Music by MATTHEW GERRARD
and ROBBIE NEVIL

Moderately fast Funk

Chad: What time is it? ___ All: Sum - mer - time.

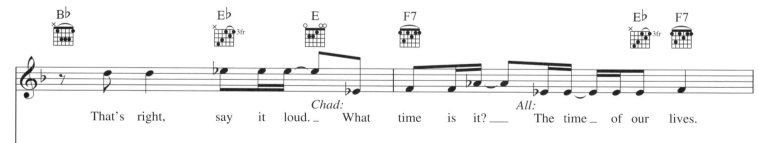

It's our va - ca - tion. What time is it? ___ Chad: All: Par - ty time.

That's right, say it loud. _ Chad: What time is it? ___ The time _ of our lives. All:

heart to take __ a chance. __ I'm here to stay, __ not mov - in' a - way, read - y

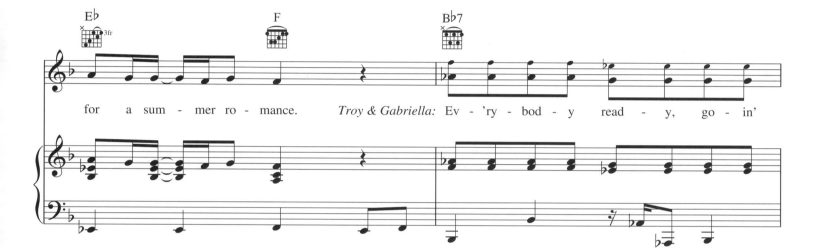

for a sum - mer ro - mance. *Troy & Gabriella:* Ev - 'ry - bod - y read - y, go - in'

cra - zy, yeah, we're out. Come on and let me hear you say it now, right now. *Chad:* What

time is it? __ *All:* Sum - mer - time. It's our va - ca - tion. *Chad:* What

ed - u - ca - tion va - ca - tion, __ and the par - ty nev - er has to stop. *Sharpay:* Got

things to do... we'll see you soon, and we're real - ly gon - na miss you all. __ Good - bye to

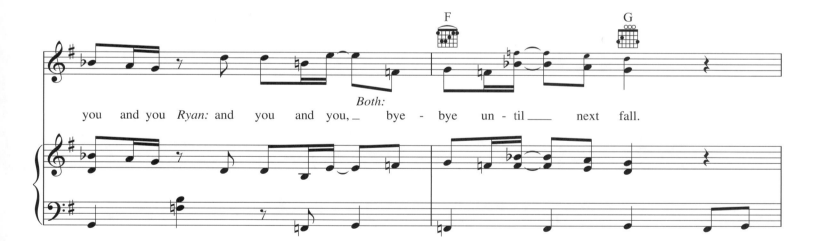

you and you *Ryan:* and you and you, __ bye - bye un - til __ next fall.

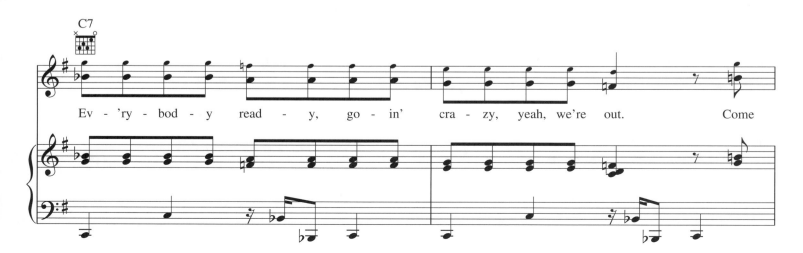

Ev - 'ry - bod - y read - y, go - in' cra - zy, yeah, we're out. Come

on and let me hear you say it now, right now. *Chad:* What time is it? __ *All:* Sum - mer - time.

Chad: It's our va - ca - tion. What time is it? __ *All:* Par - ty time.

Chad: That's right, say it loud. __ What time is it? __ *All:* The time __ of our lives.

Chad: An - ti - ci - pa - tion. What time is it? __ *All:* Sum - mer - time.

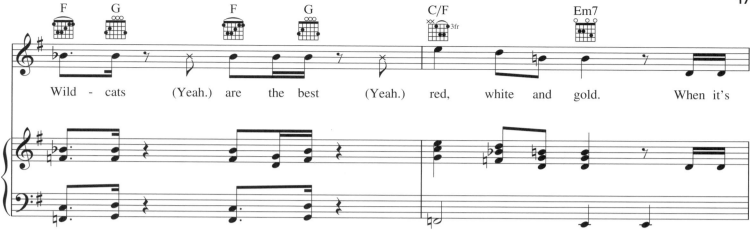

Wild - cats (Yeah.) are the best (Yeah.) red, white and gold. When it's

time to win, __ we do it (do it). We're num - ber one, __ we proved it. Let's

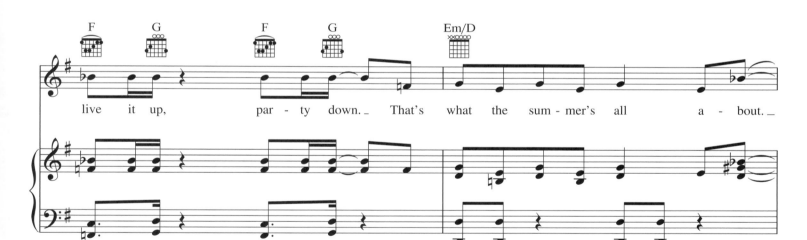

live it up, par - ty down. __ That's what the sum - mer's all a - bout. __

gliss.

All: _____ (What time is it?) __ *Gabriella:* Sum - mer - time is

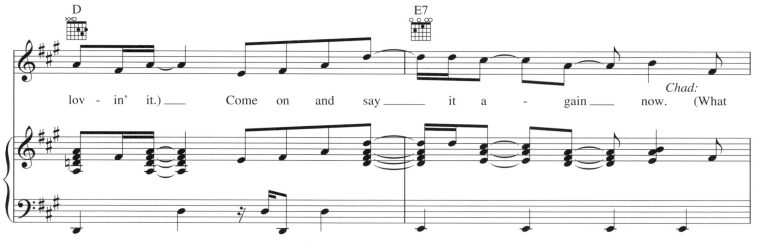

lov - in' it.) ___ Come on and say ___ it a - gain ___ now. (What

Chad:

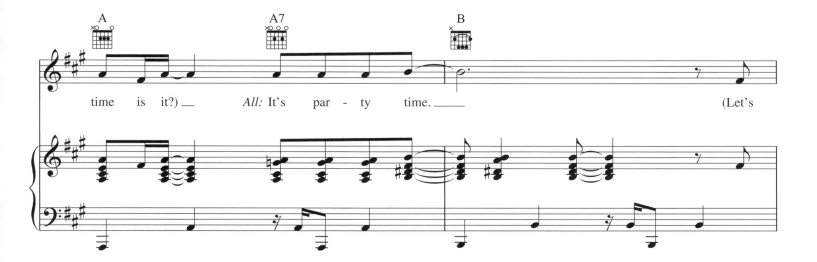

time is it?) ___ *All:* It's par - ty time. ___ (Let's

go and have) ___ the time of our lives. ___

FABULOUS

Words and Music by DAVID LAWRENCE
and FAYE GREENBERG

Freely, expressively

Sharpay: It's out with the old ___ and in with the new. ___ Good-

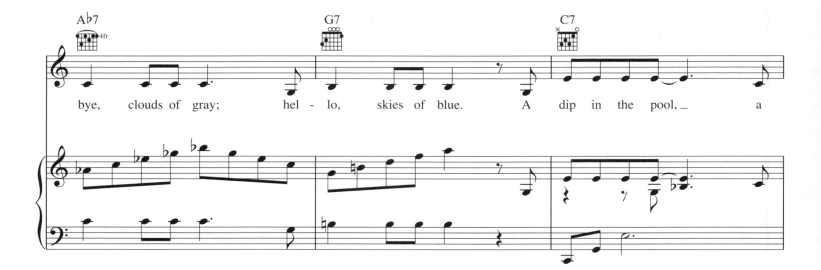

bye, clouds of gray; hel - lo, skies of blue. A dip in the pool, ___ a

trip to the spa, ___ end - less days in my chaise. The whole world ac - cord - ing to

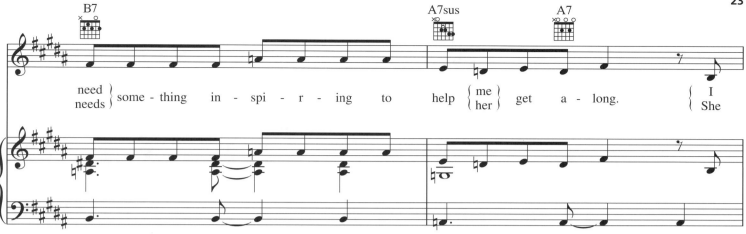

need } some-thing in-spi-r-ing to help { me } get a-long. { I
needs   her   She

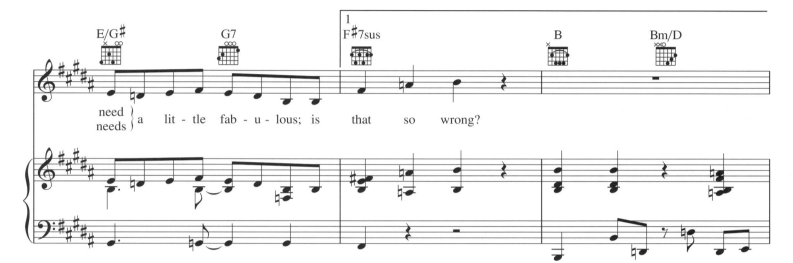

need } a lit-tle fab-u-lous; is that so wrong?
needs

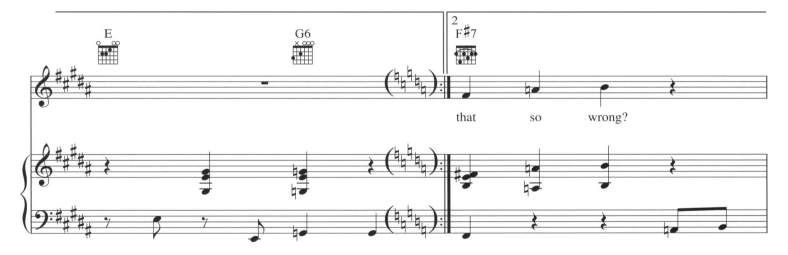

that so wrong?

Fab-u-lous pool, _ fab-u-lous splash. _ Fab-u-lous par - ties, e-ven

fab - u - lous trash. Fab - u - lous fa - shion, fab -

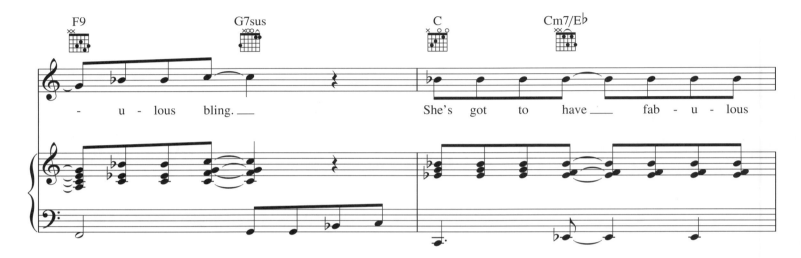

- u - lous bling.___ She's got to have___ fab - u - lous

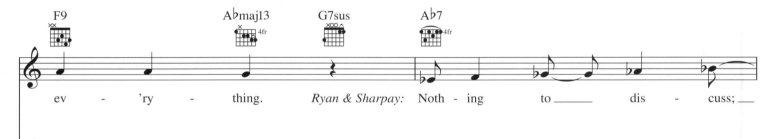

ev - 'ry - thing. *Ryan & Sharpay:* Noth - ing to___ dis - cuss;___

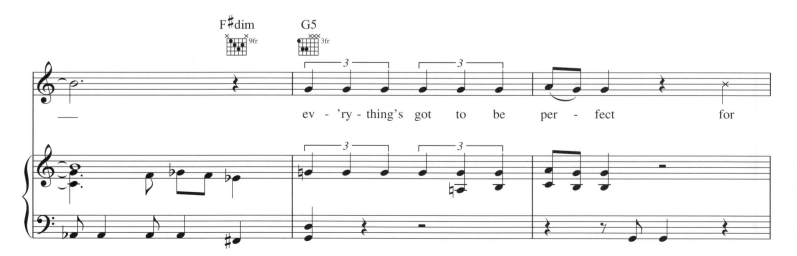

ev - 'ry - thing's got to be per - fect for

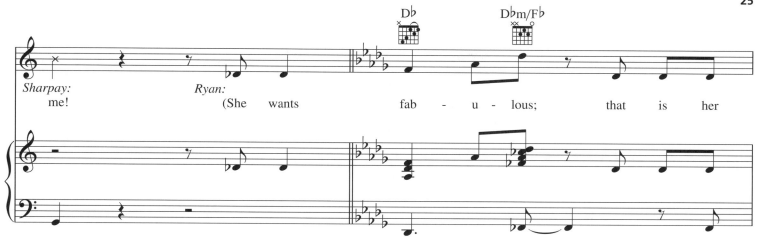

Sharpay: me! Ryan: (She wants fab - u - lous; that is her

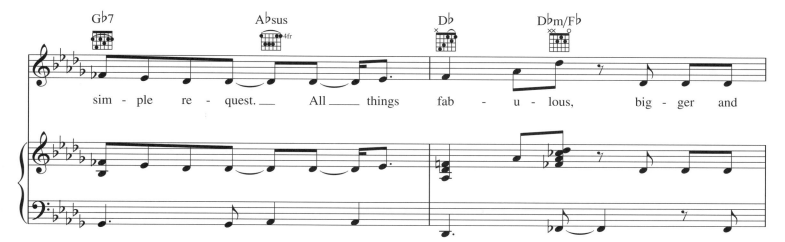

sim - ple re - quest. ___ All ___ things fab - u - lous, big - ger and

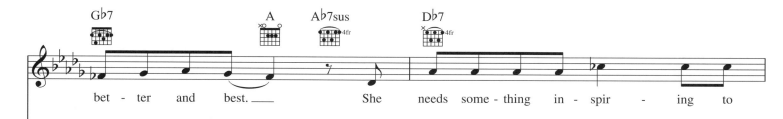

bet - ter and best. ___ She needs some - thing in - spir - ing to

help her get a - long. She needs a lit - tle fab - u - lous; is

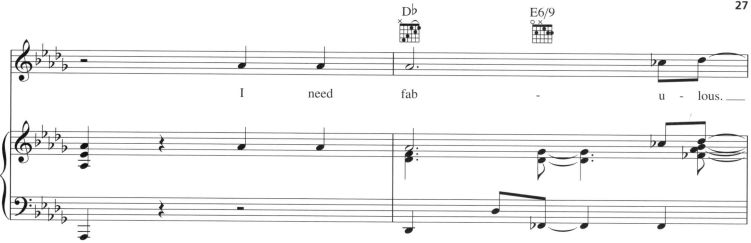

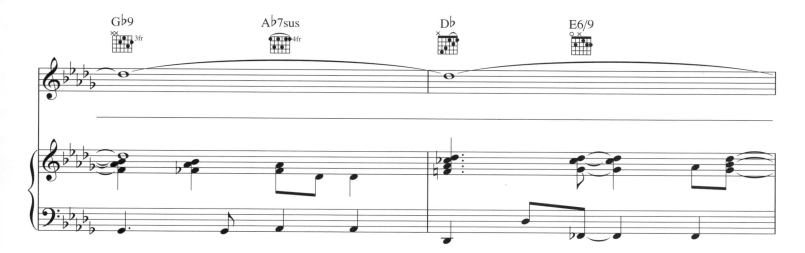

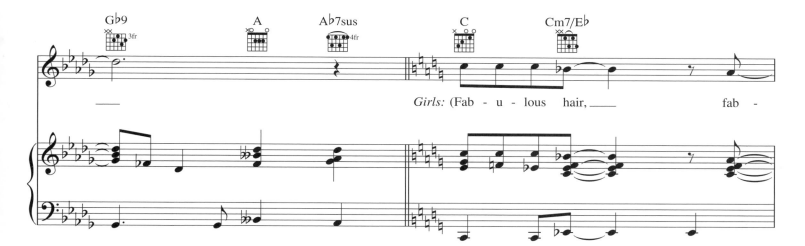

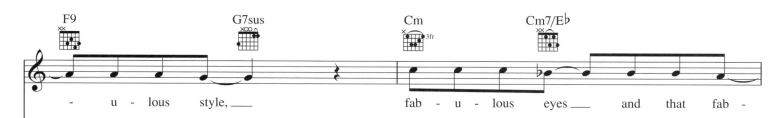

WORK THIS OUT

Words and Music by RANDY PETERSEN
and KEVIN QUINN

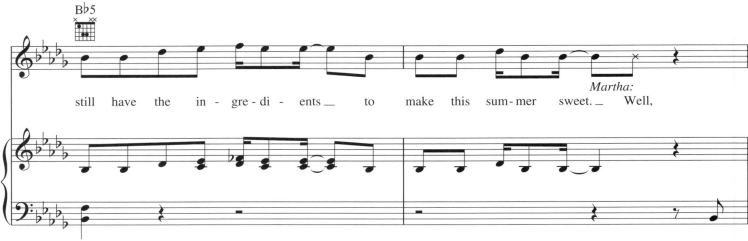

still have the in-gre-di-ents___ to make this sum-mer sweet.___ *Martha:* Well,

I got rags in-stead of rich - es, *Jason:* and all these dirt-y dish - es.

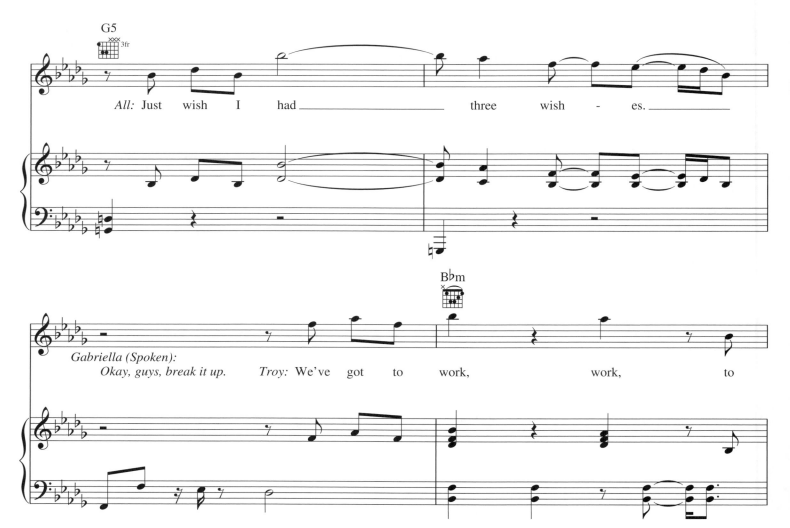

All: Just wish I had_____ three wish - es._____

Gabriella (Spoken):
Okay, guys, break it up. *Troy:* We've got to work, work, to

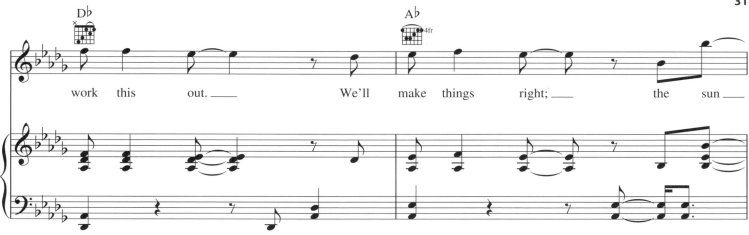

work this out. ___ We'll make things right; ___ the sun ___

___ will shine. ___ If we work, work, there'll

be no doubt. We can still save the sum - mer ___

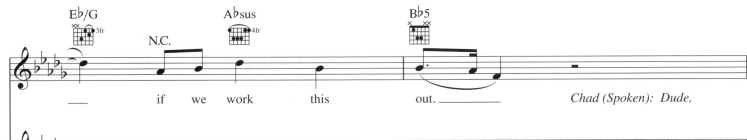

___ if we work this out. ___ *Chad (Spoken): Dude,*

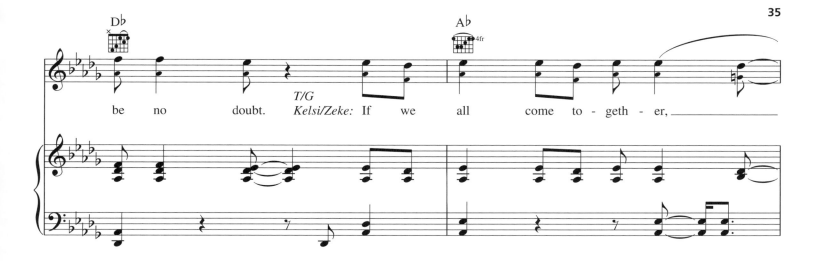

be no doubt. *Kelsi/Zeke:* If we all come to-geth-er,

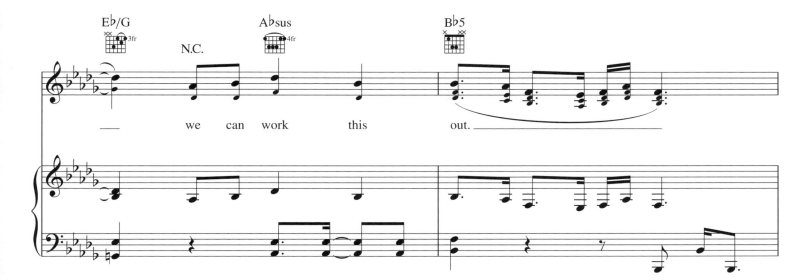

— we can work this out.

Troy: Let's work it.

Troy: Tell me what you want. _____

Gabriella: Tell me what you need. _____   *Zeke:* A lit - tle bit of sug - ar,   *Martha:* a lit - tle bit of but - ter.

Kelsi: It's the per - fect re - ci - pe. ___ (Pay-day!) *Jason:* It - 'll taste so sweet. (Pay -

day!) *Zeke:* Good e - nough to eat. *Jason:* Gon-na make some mo - tion pic - tures.

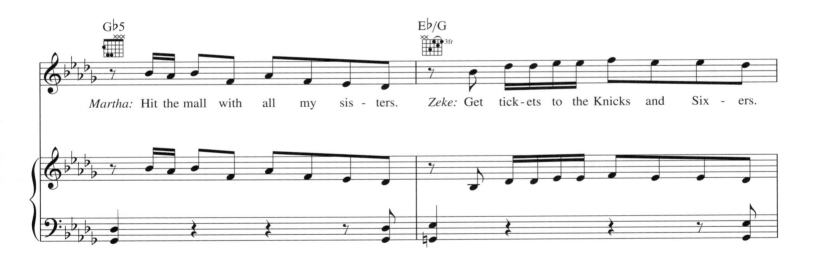

Martha: Hit the mall with all my sis - ters. *Zeke:* Get tick-ets to the Knicks and Six - ers.

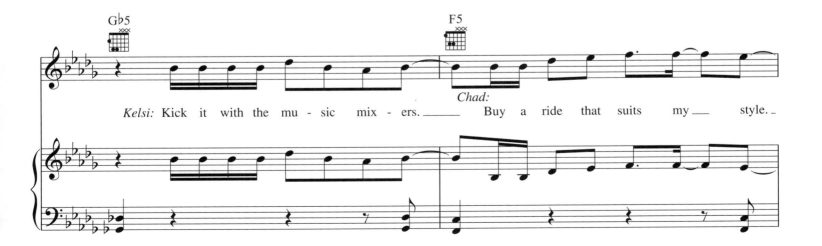

Kelsi: Kick it with the mu - sic mix - ers. ___ *Chad:* Buy a ride that suits my ___ style. ___

work, work, there'll be no doubt. We can

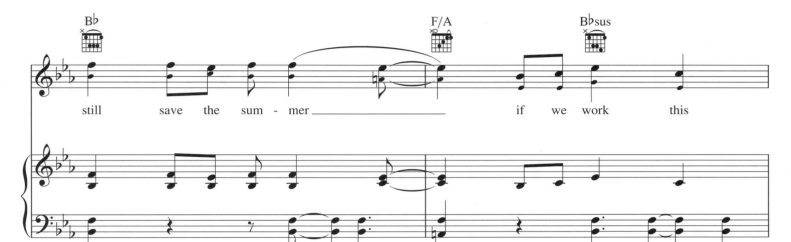

still save the sum - mer _____ if we work this

out. _____ Work ___ this, got - ta work this. _

We can ___ work ___ this out.

YOU ARE THE MUSIC IN ME

Words and Music by
JAMIE HOUSTON

Moderately fast Rock

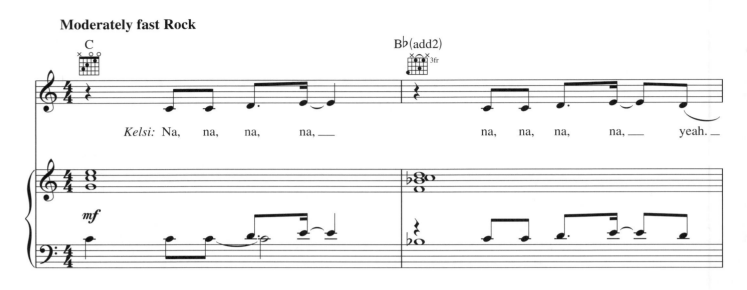

Kelsi: Na, na, na, na, ___ na, na, na, na, ___ yeah.

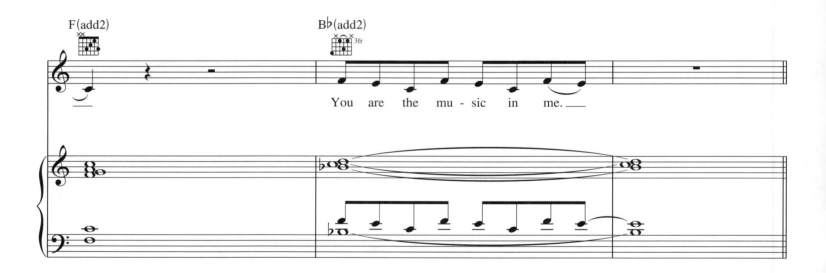

You are the mu-sic in me. ___

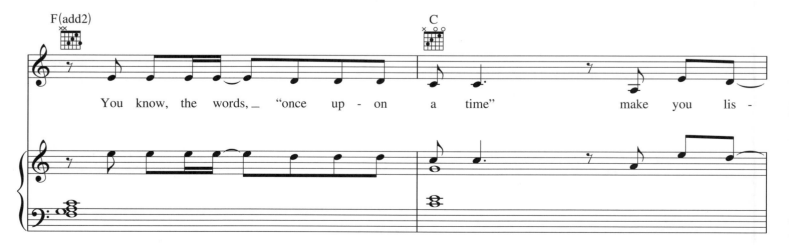

You know, the words, ___ "once up-on a time" make you lis-

ten. There's a rea - son.

Kelsi & Gabriella:
When you dream, __ there's a chance you'll find __ a lit - tle laugh -

ter or "hap - py ev - er af - ter." You're a har - mo - ny __ to the

Gabriella & Troy:

mel - o - dy __ that's ech - o - ing __ in - side __ my head. __ A sin -

Gabriella:

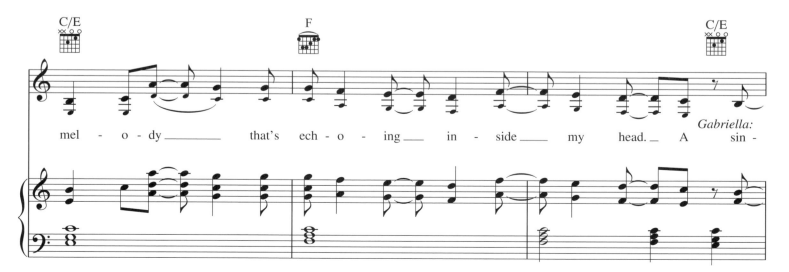

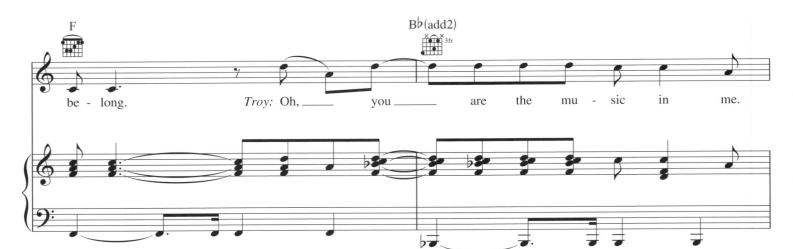

eas - y, be - cause you see the real __ me. As I *Both:* am __ you un -

- der - stand, __ and that's more than __ I've ev -

- er known. __ *Gabriella:* To hear your voice __ a - bove the noise, __ *Both:* and

know I'm not a - lone. *Gabriella:* Oh, you're sing - in' to me. __

(Me.) _____ To - geth - er we're gon - na sing. (Sing.) _____

___ We got the pow - er to say ___ *Troy:* what we feel, ___ con -

nect - ed and real, __ *Gabriella:* can't keep it all ___ in - side. ___

All: (Na, na, na, na.) (Na, na, na, na, na.) (Na, na, na, na. You__

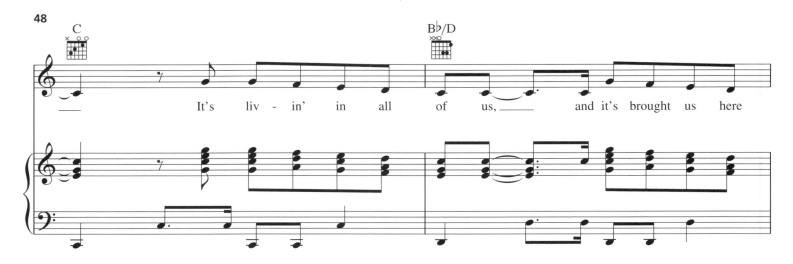

It's liv-in' in all of us, ____ and it's brought us here

be-cause you ____ are the mu-sic in me.

Na, na, na, na. Na, na, na, na, na. Na, na, na, na. You __

__ are the mu-sic in me. ____

I DON'T DANCE

Words and Music by MATTHEW GERRARD
and ROBBIE NEVIL

Energetic Funk

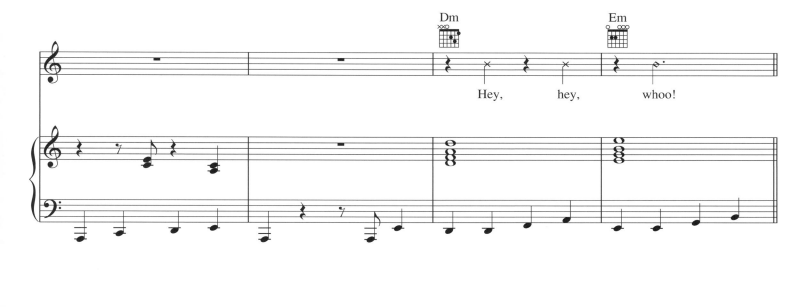

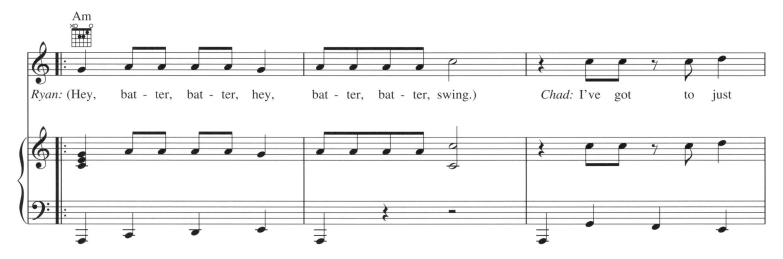

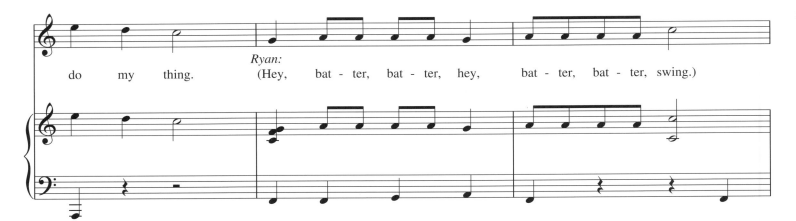

do my thing. *Ryan:* (Hey, bat-ter, bat-ter, hey, bat-ter, bat-ter, swing.)

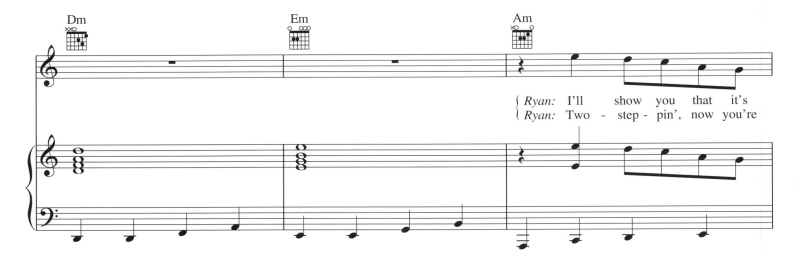

Dm   Em   Am

{ *Ryan:* I'll show you that it's
{ *Ryan:* Two - step - pin', now you're

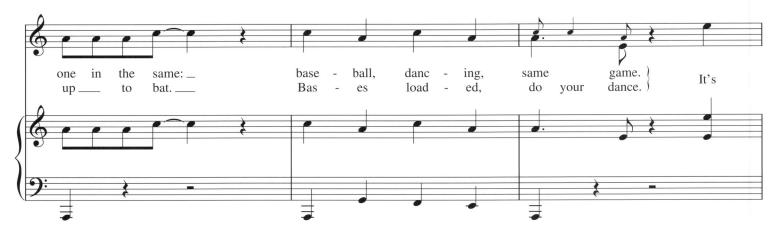

one in the same: ___ base - ball, danc - ing, same game. } It's
up ___ to bat. ___ Bas - es load - ed, do your dance. }

F   Dm

eas - y: ___ { step up ___ to the plate,
Take ___ your best shot,

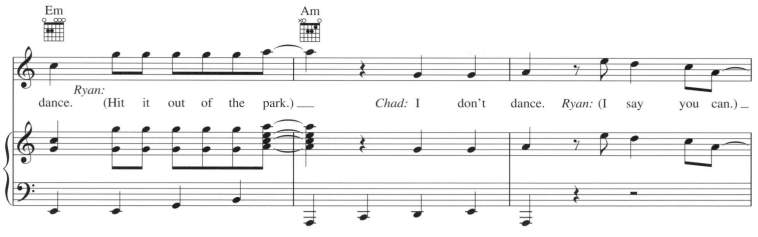

Em   Am

Ryan: dance. (Hit it out of the park.) ___ *Chad:* I don't dance. *Ryan:* (I say you can.) _

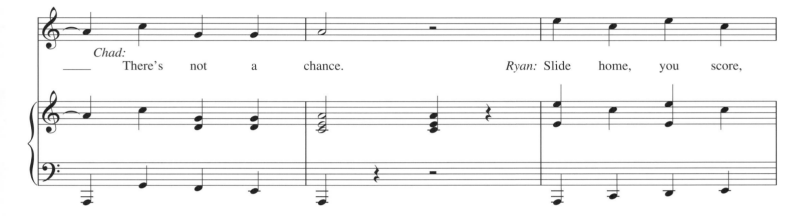

Chad: ___ There's not a chance. *Ryan:* Slide home, you score,

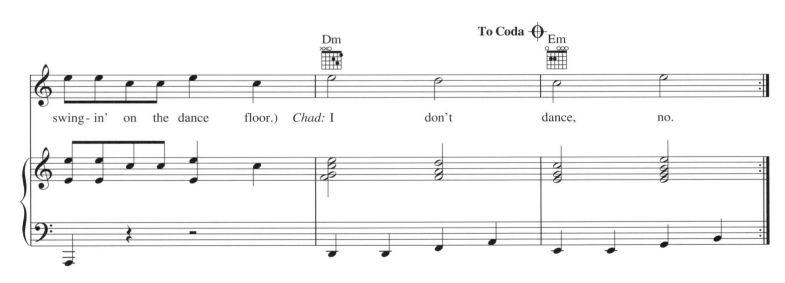

Dm   To Coda Em

swing-in' on the dance floor.) *Chad:* I don't dance, no.

N.C.

Ryan: Lean back, tuck it in, take a chance. _ Swing it out, spin a-round,

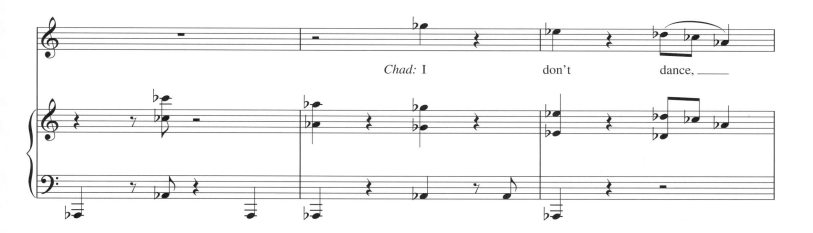

Ryan: You can do it.

Chad: I don't dance, _____

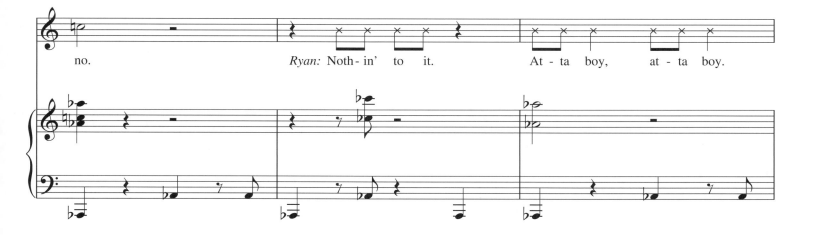

no. *Ryan:* Noth-in' to it. At - ta boy, at - ta boy.

Yeah. *Chad:* Hey, bat-ter, bat-ter, hey, bat-ter, bat-ter what.

D.S. al Coda

Ryan: One, two, three, four, ev-'ry-bod-y swing. Come on! __

CODA

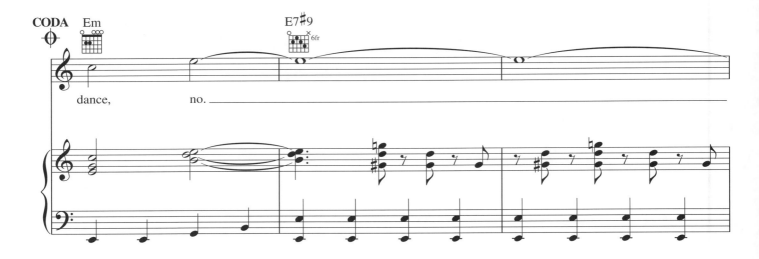

dance, no. _____

GOTTA GO MY OWN WAY

Words and Music by ADAM WATTS
and ANDY DODD

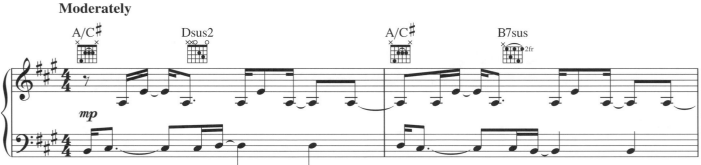

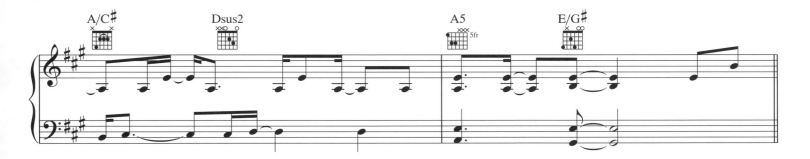

Gabriella: I got-ta say what's on ___ my mind. ___
Don't wan-na leave it all ___ be - hind, ___

Some-thing a - bout ___ us does - n't seem ___ right ___ these ___ days.
but I get ___ my hopes ___ up and I watch them ___ fall ___ ev - 'ry time.

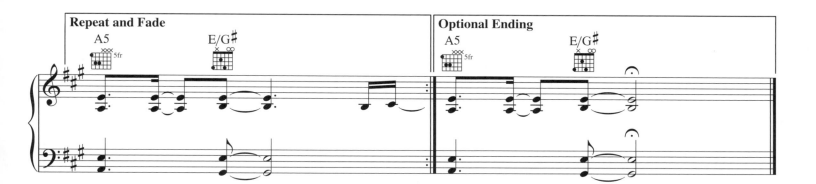

BET ON IT

Words and Music by TIM JAMES
and ANTONINA ARMATO

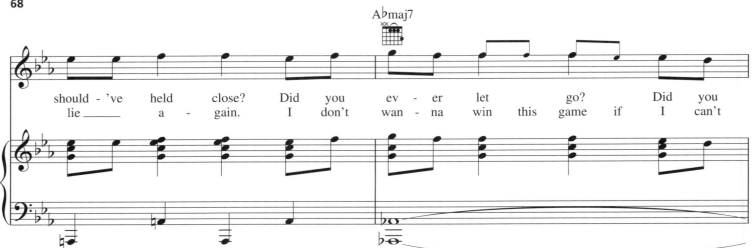

should-'ve held close? Did you ev-er let go? Did you
lie _____ a - gain. I don't wan-na win this game if I can't

ev - er not know? ____
play __ it my way. __

I'm not gon-na stop; that's who I am.

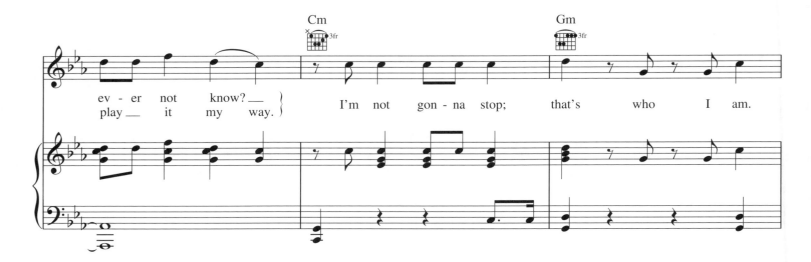

I'll give it all I got; that is __ my plan. Will I find what I lost?

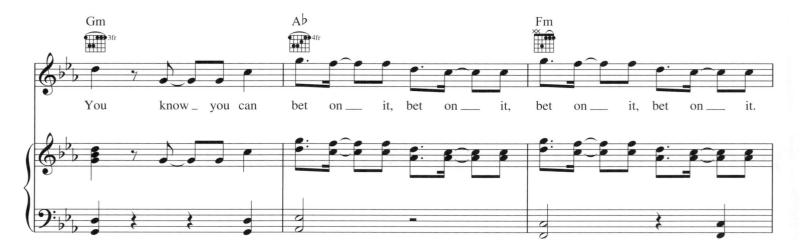

You know_ you can bet on __ it, bet on __ it, bet on __ it, bet on __ it.

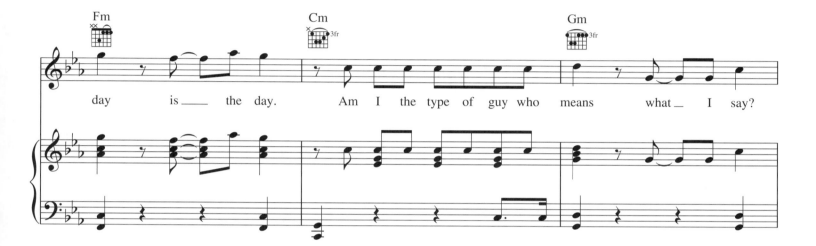

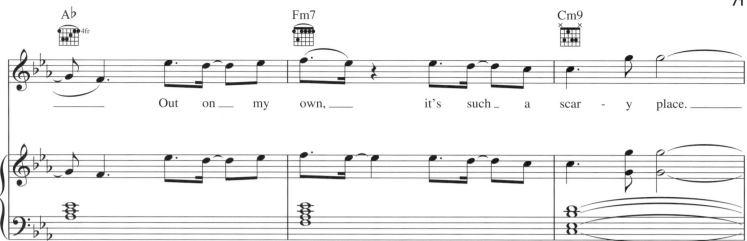

Out on my own,___ it's such a scar-y place.___

___ The an-swers___ are all in-side___ of

me.___ All I got to do___

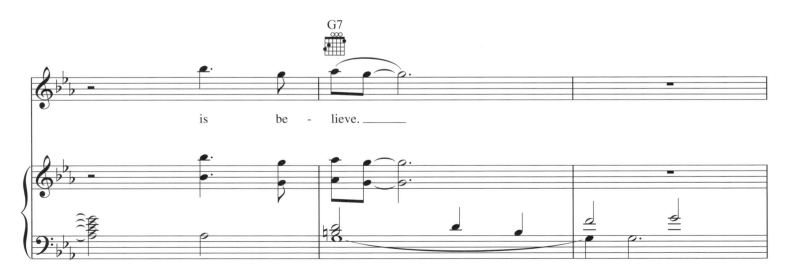

is be-lieve.___

I'm not gon-na stop, not gon-na stop till I get my shot.

That's who I am, that is my plan. We'll end up on top. You

can bet on it, bet on it, bet on it, bet on. You can ____

bet on ___ it, bet on ___ it, bet on ___ it, bet on ___ it.

I wan - na make it right; that is ___ the way

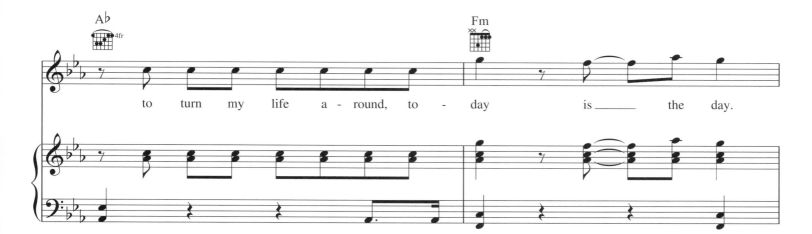

to turn my life a - round, to - day is ___ the day.

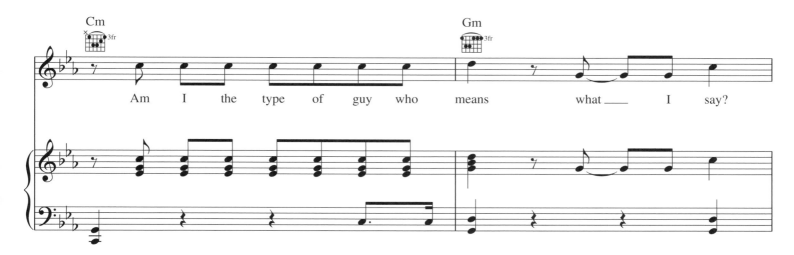

Am I the type of guy who means what ___ I say?

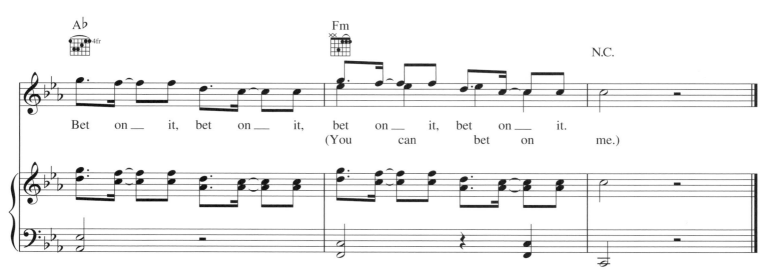

Bet on ___ it, bet on ___ it, bet on ___ it, bet on ___ it.
(You can bet on me.)

EVERYDAY

Words and Music by
JAMIE HOUSTON

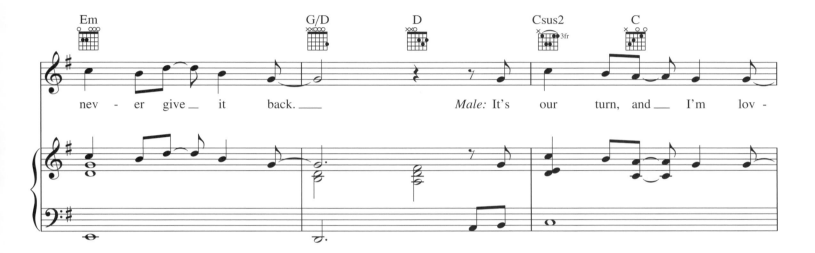

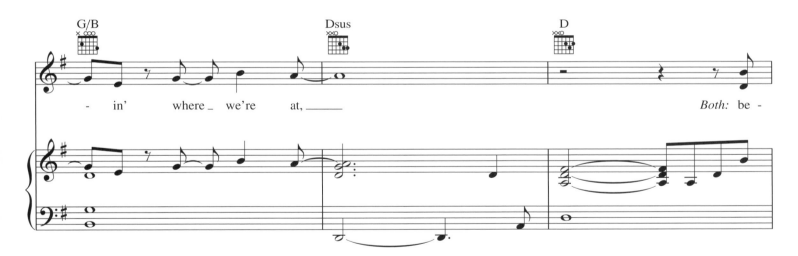

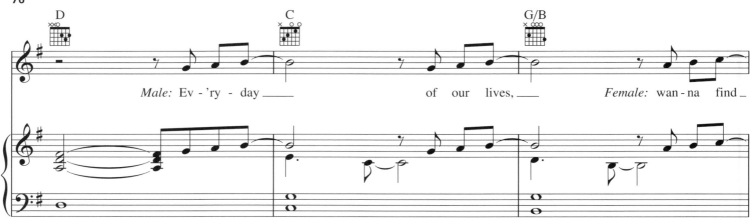

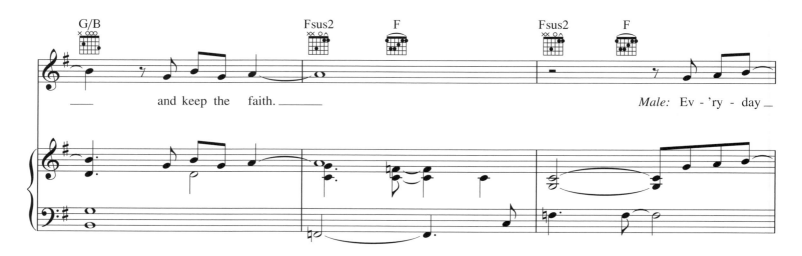

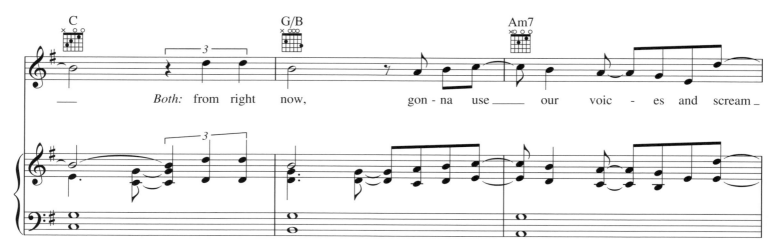

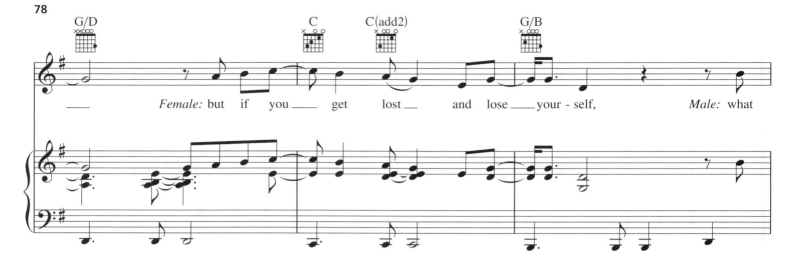

Female: but if you __ get lost __ and lose __ your - self, *Male:* what

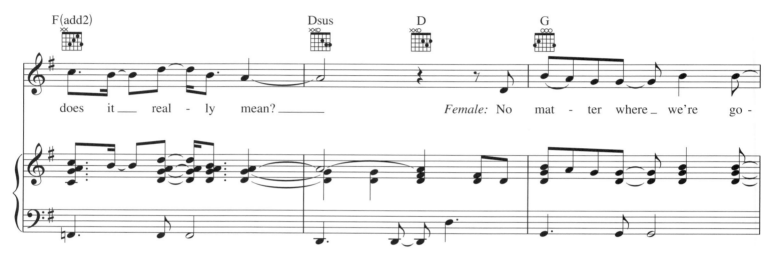

does it __ real - ly mean? _____ *Female:* No mat - ter where __ we're go -

- ing, __ *Male:* it starts from where __ we are. _____ *Female:* There's

Both:
more to life __ when we lis - ten to __ our hearts. _____

Ev-'ry-day _____ *Male:* from _ right now, _____ gon-na use _

_ our voic-es and scream _ out loud. _ Take _ my hand; to-geth-er we _

_ will cel-e-brate. _____ *Female:* Oh, _ ev-'ry-day. _____

Male: We're tak-ing it back, _ we're do-ing it here to-geth-er. It's bet-ter like that, _ and strong-er

keep the faith. _____

Choir: Ev -'ry - day ___
(Lead vocals ad lib. to end)

Cmaj9 G/B Am

___ of our lives, ___ wan - na find ___ you there, _ wan - na hold ___

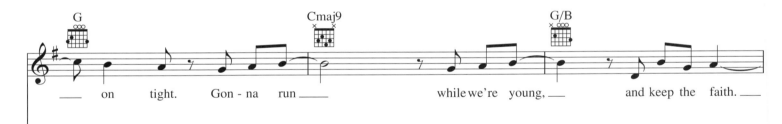

G Cmaj9 G/B

___ on tight. Gon - na run ___ while we're young, ___ and keep the faith. ___

Fmaj9 Cmaj9

___ Ev -'ry - day ___ from ___ right

now, gon-na use ___ our voic - es and scream ___ out loud. ___ Take ___ my

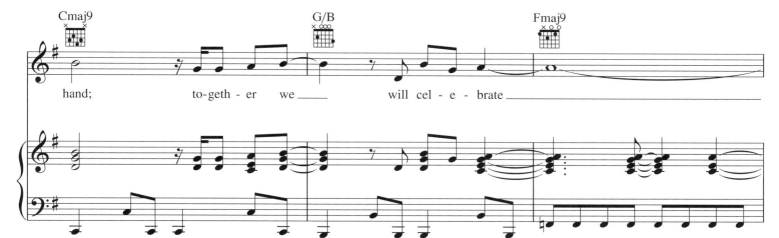

hand; to-geth - er we ___ will cel - e - brate ___

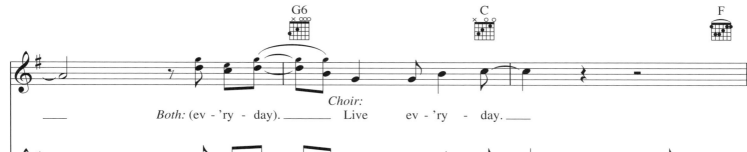

Both: (ev - 'ry - day). ___ Live ev - 'ry - day. ___

Choir:

Love ev - 'ry - day. ___ Live ev - 'ry - day. ___

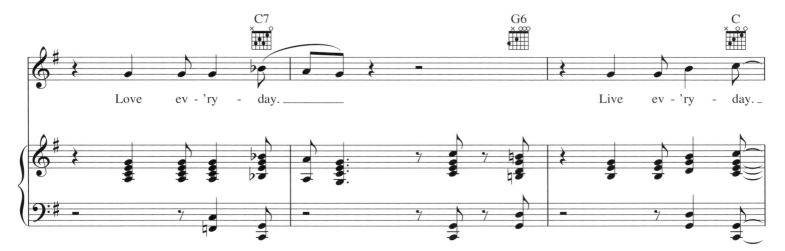

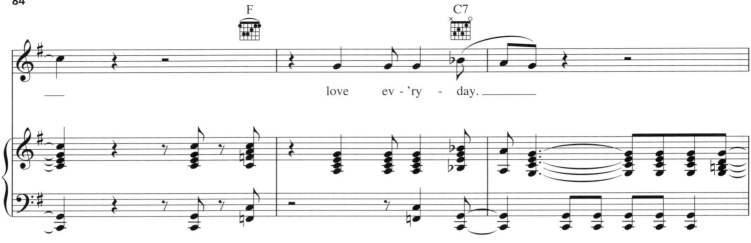

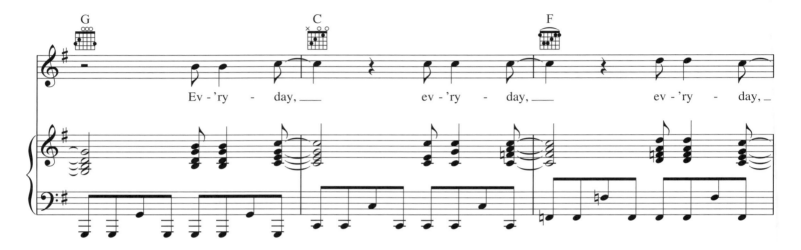

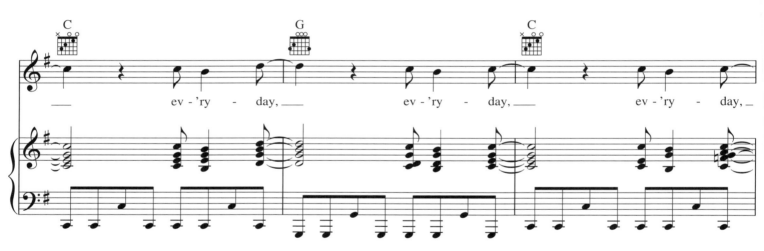

ALL FOR ONE

Words and Music by MATTHEW GERRARD
and ROBBIE NEVIL

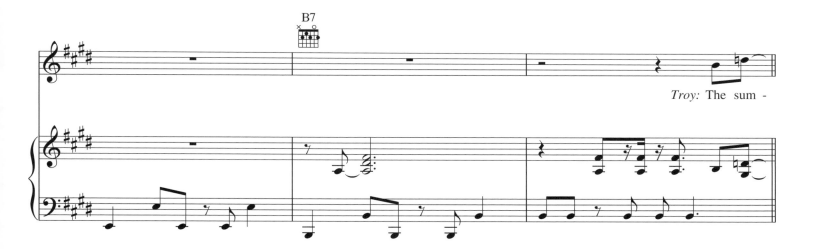

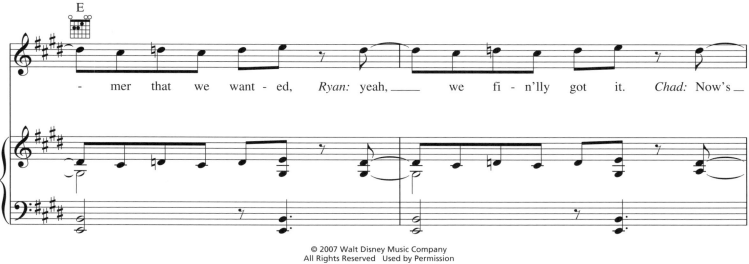

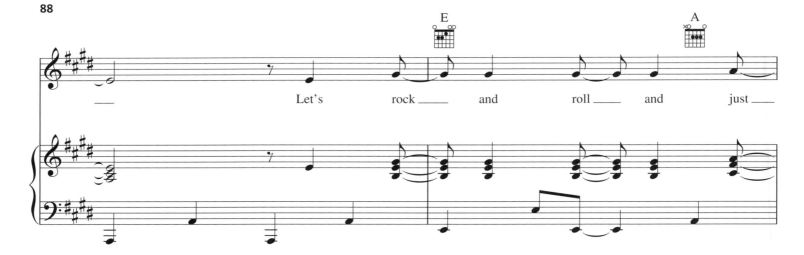

Let's rock ___ and roll ___ and just ___

___ let go, ___ feel the rhy - thm of ___ the drums. ___

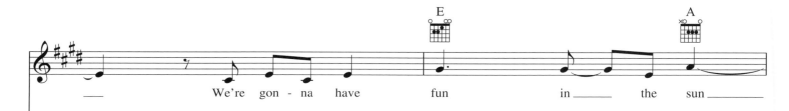

___ We're gon - na have fun in ___ the sun ___

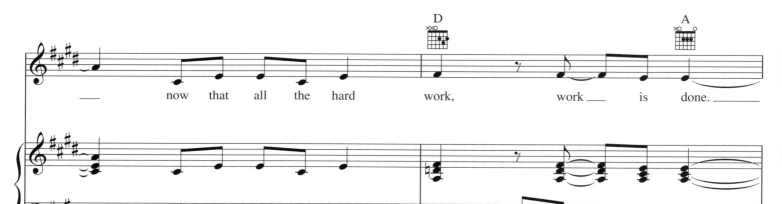

___ now that all the hard work, work ___ is done. ___

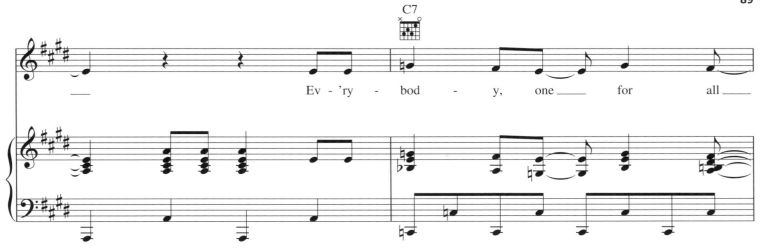

Ev-'ry-bod - y, one ____ for all ____

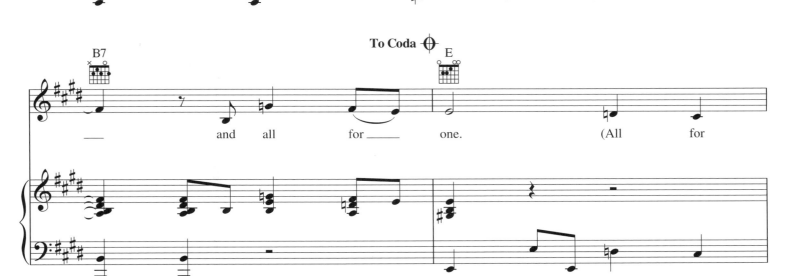

and all for ____ one. (All for

one.) (All for one, one.)

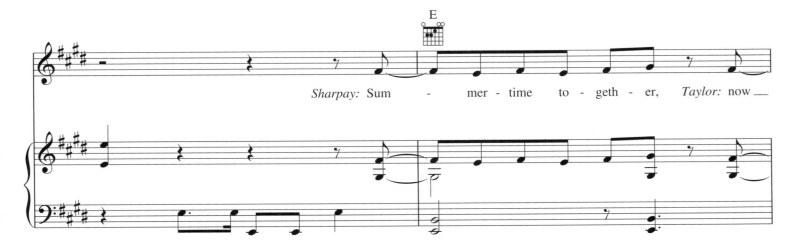

Sharpay: Sum - mer-time to-geth-er, *Taylor:* now ____

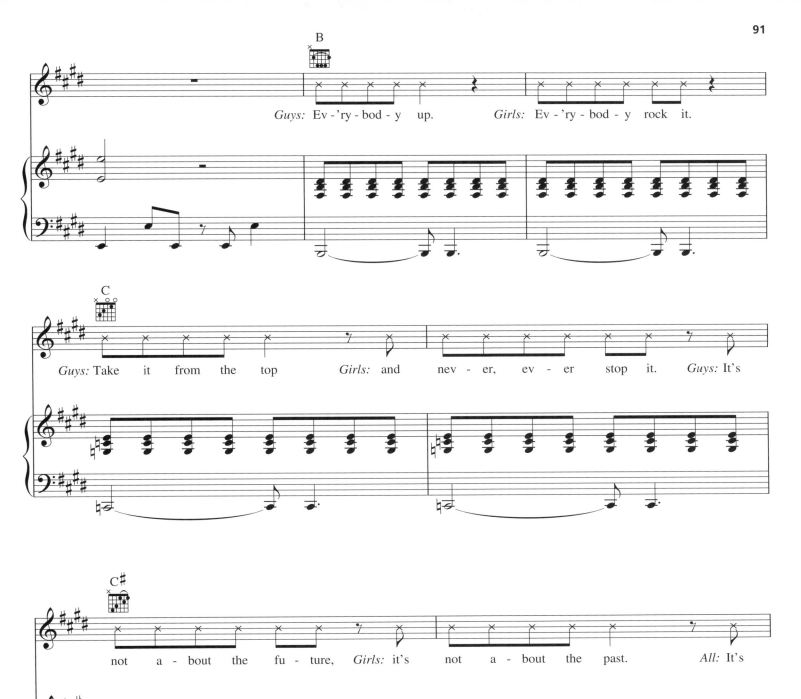

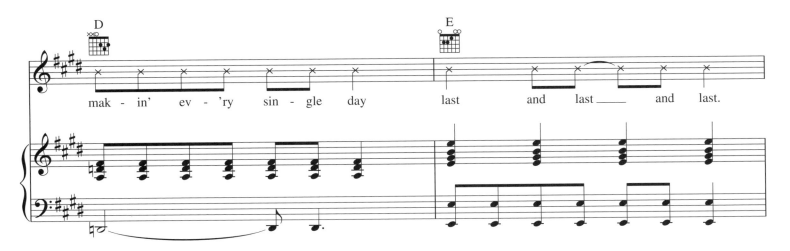

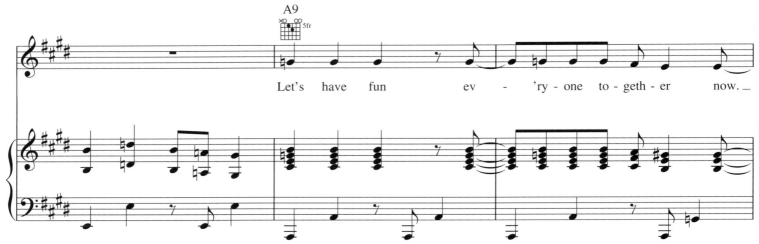

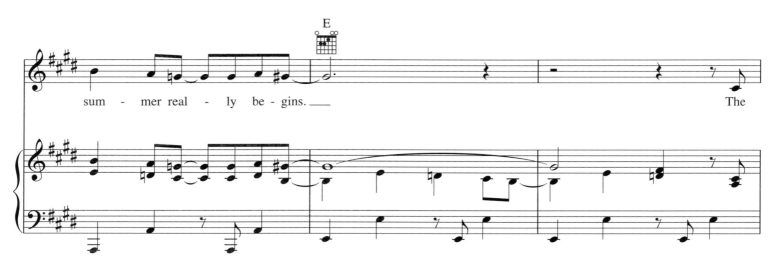

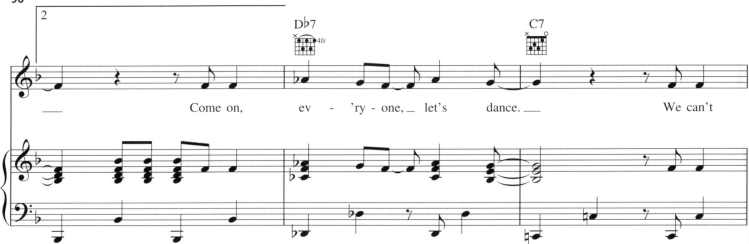

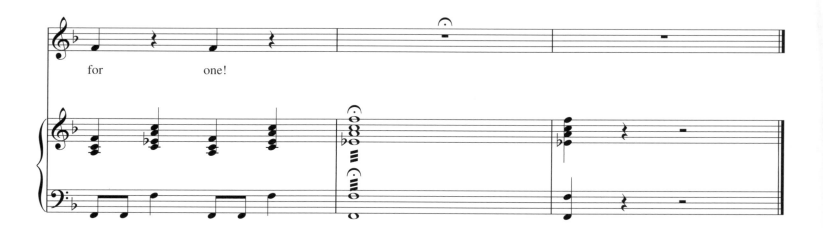

HUMU HUMU NUKU NUKU APUAA

Words and Music by DAVID LAWRENCE
and FAYE GREENBERG

Ryan: A

long time a - go in a land far a - way lived the pine - ap - ple prin - cess,
dreams of a boy who is un - der a spell that has left him all wet and

Ti - ki. She was sweet as a peach, in a pine - ap - ple way, but so
scal - y. *Sharpay:* I___ sing from my heart of the pow - er of love, just a

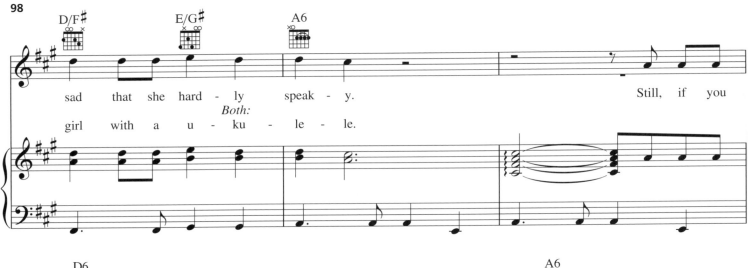

sad that she hard - ly speak - y.   Still, if you

Both:
girl with a u - ku - le - le.

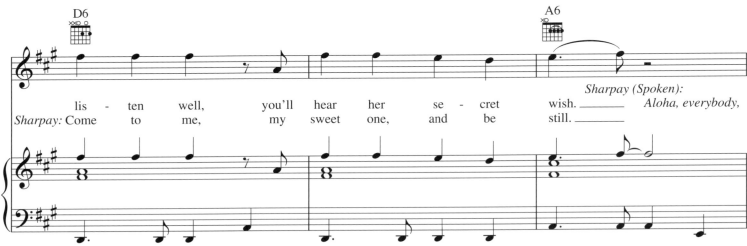

lis - ten well, you'll hear her se - cret wish. _____ *Aloha, everybody,*

Sharpay: Come to me, my sweet one, and be still. _____

Sharpay (Spoken):

my name is Tiki.   I long to free a tru - ly re - mark - a - ble

I'll grasp your tail and stroke each __ ten - der

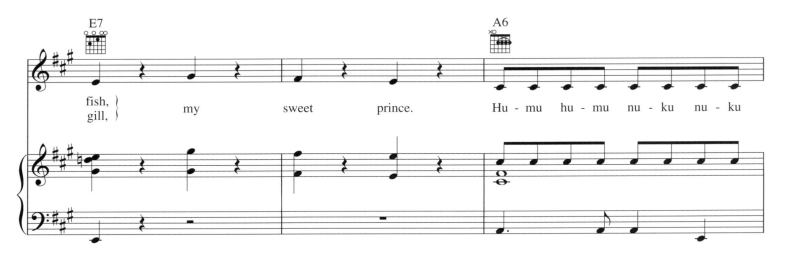

fish, }
gill, } my sweet prince. Hu - mu hu - mu nu - ku nu - ku

a - pu - a - 'a, ___ Ma - ki hi - ki ma - la - hi - ni - who. Hu -

- mu hu - mu nu - ku nu - ku a - pu - a - 'a, ooh, _____

Ha - wa - na wa - ka wa - ka wa - ka ni - ki pu pu pu.

(Spoken:) Ryan, *the fog?* *Ryan:* She

Play 4 times

fish talk... *No lie:* *(Vocal sound effects and gurgling)*

Sharpay
(Spoken): And then the fish turns into a gorgeous prince and sings, "I'm Prince

A6 E7/B

Hu - mu hu - mu nu - ku nu - ku a - pu - a - 'a, _____ a -

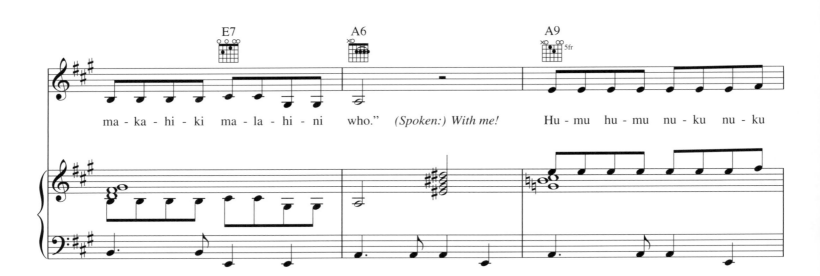

E7 A6 A9

ma - ka - hi - ki ma - la - hi - ni who." *(Spoken:) With me!* Hu - mu hu - mu nu - ku nu - ku

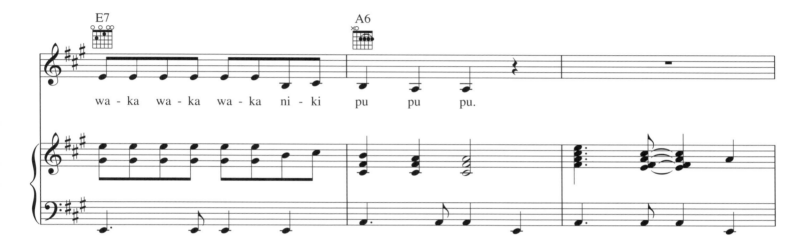

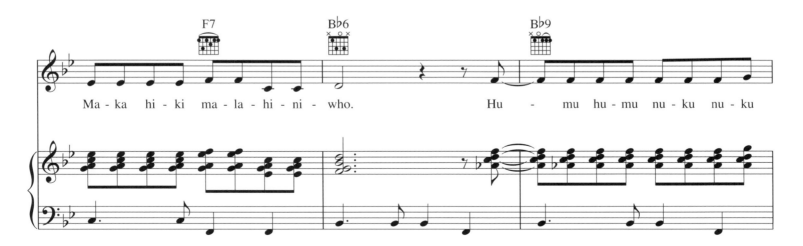

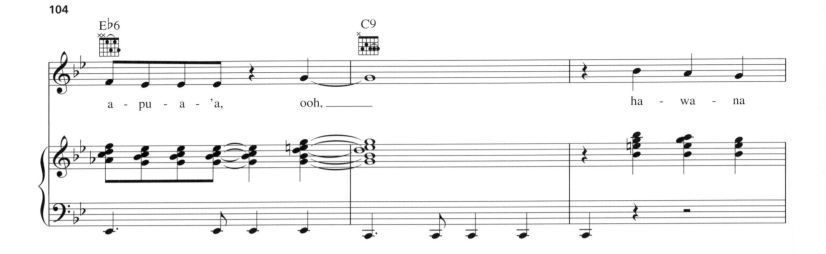

a - pu - a - 'a, ooh, _____ ha - wa - na

wa - ka wa - ka wa - ka ni - ki pu pu pu. Wa - ka wa - ka wa - ka ni - ki

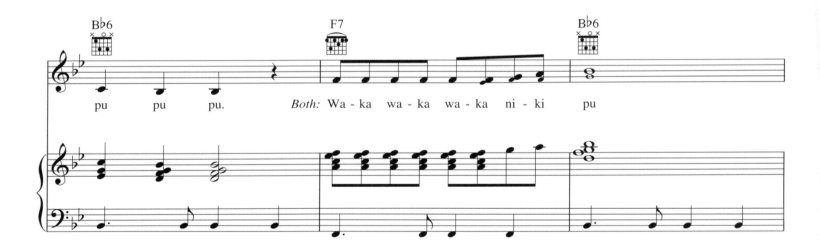

pu pu pu. *Both:* Wa - ka wa - ka wa - ka ni - ki pu

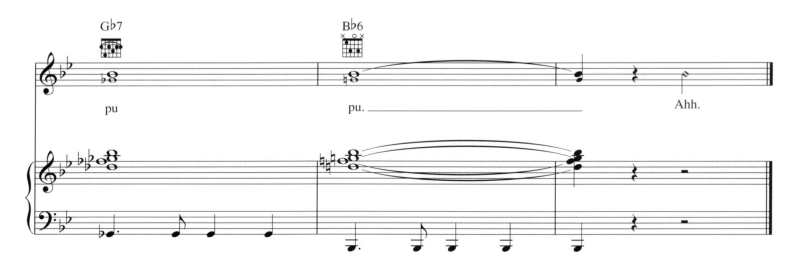

pu pu. _____ Ahh.